ANGKOR

D0095586

The author
Dawn Rooney, who was born in the United States, has spent many years researching art history in Southeast Asia. Awarded a Ph D in Art History in 1983, she has written several books on Southeast Asian art and culture and contributed articles to many magazines, including *National Geographic* and *Oriental Art.*

The photographer
In 1971, photographer Michael Freeman took a break from advertizing to photograph the Amazon for Time-Life Books, and never looked back. He has made Southeast Asia his area of expertize and been published in numerous magazines, including *Geo* and *National Geographic*, as well as in a number of books. *Angkor: The Hidden Glories* is his most recent work.

Note on pronunciation of Sanskrit words
r is pronounced as *ri* in *ri*ver eg Kṛṣṇa [Krishna]
c is pronounced as *ch* in *ch*urch
n is pronounced as *ng* in so*ng*
s is pronounced *sh* eg Śeṣa [Shesha]

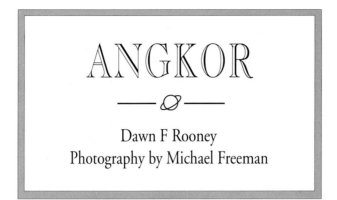

ANGKOR

Dawn F Rooney
Photography by Michael Freeman

PASSPORT BOOKS
a division of *NTC Publishing Group*
Lincolnwood, Illinois USA

Published by Passport Books in conjunction with
The Guidebook Company Limited

This edition first published in 1994 by Passport Books, a division of NTC Publishing Group,
4255 W. Touhy Avenue, Lincolnwood (Chicago), Illinois 60646-1975, USA,
originally published by The Guidebook Company Ltd.

ISBN: 0-8442-9888-3
Library of Congress Catalog Card Number: 93–84763

Editor: Susan Faircloth
Series Editor: Anna Claridge
Illustrations Editor: Caroline Robertson
Design: De•Style Studio
Map Design: Bai Yiliang

Front cover by Michael Freeman
Illustrations supplied courtesy of Antiques of the Orient, Singapore, from the Garnier Plates
collection 5, 30–31, 36–37, 64, 65, 67, 89, 90–91 (above), 93, 107; Bibliothèque Nationale,
Paris 105, 134; Michael Freeman 12, 18–19, 39, 43, 47, 50, 55, 59, 74, 78–79, 102, 138–139,
178–179, 201, 212, 234; Tim Hall 130, 224; Private Collection 220; Dawn Rooney 84, 94, 100,
101, 128, 142, 150, 151, 163, 172, 193; Wattis Fine Art 8, 26–27, 70–71, 98, 136–137

Production House: Twin Age Limited, Hong Kong
Printed in Hong Kong

The ascent to one of the five towers at Angkor Wat,
Voyage d'Exploration en Indo-Chine, *Francis Garnier, 1873*

'Finally the frontiers are opening up for Cambodian people and Cambodia will find its place again in the world.' French President François Mitterand spoke these historic words on 23 October 1991 in Paris at the official signing of a political settlement ending the war in Cambodia. An early effect of this renewed hope for peace and unity was the re-opening, after nearly two decades, of one of the world's greatest cultural heritages—Angkor.

Rāhu, a demon with no body or claws

Contents

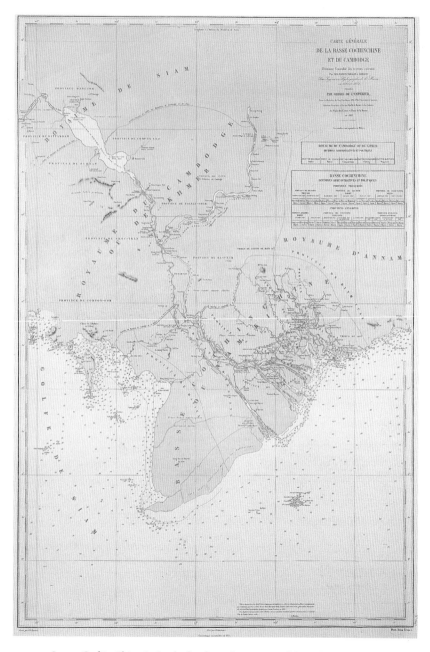

Lower Cochin China & Cambodia, *drawn by Manen, Vidalin and Heraud, 1875*

Preface

—*Amanda Reynolds*

When the author, Dr Dawn F Rooney, first visited Angkor in 1969, she arrived as a tourist armed only with curiosity and enthusiasm to see one of the world's great cultural heritages.

The flight from Bangkok to Siem Reap passed over the temple complex allowing passengers a superb bird's eye view of Angkor Wat. Awestruck by its sheer size and complexity, Dr Rooney felt for the first time the mesmerizing effect of the fabled temples. At dusk, on the terrace of the French-built Auberge des Temps, she gazed across at Angkor Wat, watching the majestic temple towers lit by the rays of a setting sun. That moment, she wrote, 'pierced my soul'.

A week-long exploration of temples increased her fascination. The architecture, accentuated by exquisite decorative detail and powerful sculpture, she said, 'transcended the boundaries of anticipated beauty'. 'I had never seen such mysterious, enigmatic yet human and harmonious art.'

Nevertheless more than twenty years were to pass between the author's first and second trips to Angkor as the eruption of civil unrest led to the closure of the temples to tourists from 1969 to 1991. In that time Dr Rooney devoted herself to the study of Khmer art and civilization, especially the ceramics of the era which she has made her area of expertise. Travels to kiln sites in northeastern Thailand, within the territorial boundaries of the Khmer Empire between the eleventh and thirteenth centuries, yielded material for a PhD dissertation and two books on Khmer ceramics.

A peace agreement in October 1991 led to the re-opening of Angkor. On her return that year, and many trips since, Dr Rooney found the hiatus has eroded none of the temples' mystique. Although the facilities for tourists are increasing all the time—more hotels, restaurants, food and cold drinks at the sites—the monuments remain mercifully unchanged. They continue, at least for the moment, to be easily accessible, uncrowded and in undisturbed surroundings. One major problem remains the depredations of looters who are depriving Angkor of archaeological evidence and selling the cultural relics on the international art market.

Angkor, she has noted, is most dramatic at sunset, sunrise and in the moonlight. Seeing the temples by the light of a full moon is still an unsurpassed experience. Her favourite time of year for visiting the complex is during the rainy season. 'To me, the background of the verdant vegetation against the grey sandstone and reddish brick of the temples is a magical combination.'

Travellers using this book as a guide to the monuments will find their experience heightened by its detailed scholarship, avid armchair tourists will discover in its pages an irresistible read. Above all, the author's enthusiasm will inspire many more people to visit this captivating place.

PART I

BACKGROUND

Introduction

The tale of it is incredible; the wonder which is Angkor is unmatched in Asia.[1]

The temples startle with their splendour and perfection but beyond the emotions they evoke lie complex microcosms of the universe steeped in cosmology. While a thorough understanding may be out of reach for many, the monuments' profound effect touches everyone. Even though there is little doubt the temples of India served as models for Angkor initially, there are concepts found in Khmer structures that are rare in India. Ideas such as the association of architecture with a capital, the link between the ruler and a divinity, the symbolism of the pyramid temple with a cosmic mountain are all Khmer concepts manifested in the monuments. The sculpture is equally as individualistic. Sensuous, yet never erotic, male and female forms stand in grandeur and dignity offering universal appeal, past and present.

This book is both an introduction and a guide to Angkor. It is an effort to bring together in a single volume the information on Angkor that would be useful for an appreciation of the monuments. The text has been compiled from published sources, mainly works by Lawrence P Briggs and Maurice Glaize.[2] It consists of two parts: the first gives background information on various aspects of the Khmer civilization and is designed for reading before a visit to Angkor while the second concentrates on the monuments and is intended for use as a guide to the sites.

The first part begins with the geography of Cambodia. Historical details follow, tracing the Khmers from early times through the period of Angkor to the rediscovery of the ruins by foreigners. The final part of the history section describes modern developments at Angkor, touching on restoration work that has been done on the monuments, the state of the temples today, and intended conservation for the future. A chapter on religion discusses the beliefs and cults of the Khmers, identifies the principal deities and mythical beings, and summarizes the legends of the most frequently depicted scenes on reliefs. The next chapter, on Khmer art, discusses the materials, architectural elements, plans and decoration, touches on the cosmological significance of the monuments, and ends with a description of the various art styles of architecture and sculpture.

The second half of the book serves as a reference to the monuments. It is arranged alphabetically by place according to the generally accepted name and each

---

[1]   H Churchill Candee, *Angkor, The Magnificent, The Wonder City of Ancient Cambodia* (H F & G Witherby, London, 1925), p. vii.

[2]   Lawrence Briggs 'The Ancient Khmer Empire', *Transactions of the American Philosophical Society*, 41, pt 1, 1951; Maurice Glaize, *Les Monuments du Groupe d'Angkor: Guide*, 3rd ed (A Maisonneuve, Paris, 1963).

(preceding page)
Bas-relief detail of a mythical lion in the centre and a multi-headed serpent on the left

one is treated separately, usually with an accompanying plan of the layout. A suggested route for viewing the site is marked on the plan where it is appropriate. Each description gives the location, access, date of the monument, name of the king associated with the construction, prevailing religion at the time the site was built, art style, background and layout.

Appendices include: suggested itineraries to suit the time available to see the sites, a comparative chronology of Khmer and world history, and a list of the kings. There is also a general glossary and a list of books for further reading. Finally, a detailed index allows maximum use of the book.

A general misconception of Angkor leads some people to think it is only one temple—Angkor Wat. This erroneous idea probably arose because it is the one most frequently visited and written about. Angkor, though, covers an area of 310 square kilometres (120 square miles) and comprises over 1,000 temples. Many of these have collapsed and only traces of others remain. The ground around others has not yet been cleared. This guidebook includes descriptions of the 39 accessible sites.

Measurements are in metric units with imperial units in parenthesis. The abbreviation 'BC' follows all dates before the Christian era. Dates of the Christian era have no abbreviation except where its absence would be confusing.

The use of foreign words has been avoided wherever possible and an English equivalent substituted. Technical terms have also been kept to a minimum. Where it has been necessary to use Indian-derived names such as those of deities, kings and geographical places, Sanskrit spelling based on the *Iconographic Dictionary of the Indian Religions: Hinduism, Buddhism, Jainism* by G Liebert has been adopted for consistency.[3] The phonetic system developed by the Royal Institute of Thailand has been followed for the spelling of Thai words. The Pinyin system has been used for the transliteration of Chinese words except in quotations or captions where the original text has been retained. In those instances, the Pinyin equivalent is provided in parenthesis. Khmer words conform to a phonetic spelling in English. The spelling of foreign words in quotations is sometimes inconsistent with the conventions adopted for this book because each European country spelt Asian words according to its own interpretation of sound. Diacritical marks have been used whenever possible. Foreign words are italicized unless they are proper nouns or have been adopted into the English language.

Go to Angkor, my friend, to its ruins and to its dreams.[4]

[3]   Gosta Liebert, *Iconographic Dictionary of the Indian Religions: Hinduism, Buddhism, Jainism*, Vol V in J E van Lohuizen de Leeuw (ed), *Studies in South Asian Culture*, edited for the Institute of South Asian Archaeology, University of Amsterdam (E J Brill, Leiden, 1976).

[4]   P Jeannerat de Beerski, *Angkor, Ruins in Cambodia* (Houghton Mifflin, Boston & New York, 1924), p 20.

Cambodia

N

THAILAND

LAOS

VIETNAM

DANGREK MOUNTAINS

Samrong

Koh Ker

Sisophon

Angkor
(Ruins)

Siem Reap

• Stung Treng

Battambang

Roluos

Tonlé Sap

Mekong River

Pursat

Kampong
Chhnang

Tonlé Sap River

• Kratie

CARDAMOM MOUNTAINS

Kampong
Cham

PHNOM PENH

ELEPHANT MOUNTAINS

Gulf of Thailand

Sihanouk
Ville

• Kampot

Mekong River

**HO CHI MINH
CITY**

• Oc Eo

© The Guidebook Company Ltd

South China Sea

BURMA

LAOS

*Bay of
Bengal*

THAI-
LAND

*South
China
Sea*

CAMBODIA

VIETNAM

MALAYSIA

*Indian
Ocean*

SINGA-
PORE

BRUNEI

Sumatra

INDONESIA

0	25	50	75	100	125 km
0		25		50	75 miles

Geographical Setting

Kampuchea, Cambodia, Khmer and Angkor are all names associated with a single Asian civilization renowned for its art and architecture. Kambujadesa or Kambuja was the name of the country in Sanskrit inscriptions, derived from a tribe in north India associated with Kambu Svayambhuva, the legendary founder of the Khmer civilization. Kampuchea, the modern legacy, was part of the official title of the country as recently as 1989. Cambodia, the name of this Southeast Asian country today, is an English version of Cambodge, the French name for the country. Both words are Western pronunciations of Kambuja. The inhabitants are Khmers or Cambodians; the national language is Khmer; and in the past they called their country Khmer.

The modern capital of Cambodia is Phnom ('mountain') Penh, located in the south, and the ancient capital of Angkor ('city' or 'capital') was situated 320 kilometres (199 miles) north of Phnom Penh in Siem Reap province. The name Angkor, first used by Westerners, is probably a mispronunciation of the Khmer word Nakhon, which was derived from *nāgara*, a Sanskrit word. It refers to a particular time and place in Khmer history. Angkor is used as a designation for the period of the Khmer Empire from AD 802 to 1432 and also as a general term for the monuments built during that time in the vicinity of Siem Reap. The town of Siem Reap ('the defeat of the Siamese'), the provincial capital of the province, is six kilometres (four miles) from the temple of Angkor Wat.

Cambodia comprises 181,000 square kilometres (69,884 square miles) and is bordered by Laos and Thailand on the north, Vietnam on the south and east, and the Gulf of Thailand on the west. This region corresponds to the present area of mainland Southeast Asia (see map opposite). Cambodia occupies the southwestern part of the mainland and lies midway between China and India. Its geographical position and the internal topography have influenced the cultural, social and political development of its inhabitants throughout history.

The core of the Khmer Empire remained in the vicinity of Angkor for over 500 years but the area of settlement and political domination fluctuated. At the height of territorial expansion, in the eleventh and twelfth centuries, the Khmer Empire claimed control over major parts of neighbouring countries. Substantial evidence of a former Khmer presence exists in Thailand (see map page 24). Phimai, in Nakhon Ratchasima province, was a Khmer centre wielding control over central and northeastern Thailand. It was linked to Angkor by a laterite highway extending over 225 kilometres (140 miles).

CLIMATE

Cambodia lies in a tropical zone between ten and 14° of latitude north of the equator.

View of Angkor from Phnom Bakheng

The temperature is fairly uniform throughout the year and averages 25° centigrade (77° fahrenheit). The relative humidity is higher at night and usually in excess of 90 per cent; during the day the average humidity is 80 per cent.

The monsoon cycle dictates the climate. Alternating high and low pressure over the mainland causes two monsoonal shifts that result in two seasons and a short transitional period. Between February and April, a northeastern wind blows from the continental mass of Asia across Cambodia bringing the dry, or hot, season. A southwestern wind from the Indian Ocean brings heavy rains during the wet, or rainy, season from May to October. The average annual rainfall in the delta area is 127 to 190 centimetres (50 to 75 inches). A transitional period between the wet and dry seasons occurs from November to January and is known as the cool season.

TOPOGRAPHY

The surrounding mountain ranges and internal water system of Cambodia have formed large valleys that became centres of settlement. The Cardamom Mountains (Chuor Phnom Kravanh) in the southwest have an elevation of 1,772 metres (5,814

feet) and are the highest in the country. The Elephant Range (Chuor Phnom Damrei) in the south has an elevation of 915 metres (3,002 feet). The lowest range is the Dangrek (Chuor Phnom Dangrek) which runs east–west across the north of Cambodia and has an elevation of 488 metres (1,601 feet). Between the western part of the Dangrek and the northern part of the Cardamom mountains an extension of the delta connects with lowlands in Thailand and allows communication between the two areas by land. This geographical feature played an important part in the history of the Khmers.

The Mekong River and its tributaries dominate the water system. From its source in Tibet the Mekong flows southeasterly across Cambodia from north to south. It divides into two main forks at Phnom Penh. Further divisions and channels provide river access to the interior of Cambodia and carry the waters of the Mekong south through mainland Southeast Asia until they finally discharge in the South China Sea.

The Tonle Sap (Great Lake) lies south of Angkor. 'The sea of fresh water', as it is called by natives, is an immense lake 140 kilometres (87 miles) long. The Tonle Sap River links the Mekong River to the southern end of the Great Lake. An unusual characteristic of this river is that its water flow changes direction to flow in reverse. The source of this phenomenon is the Himalaya Mountains of Central Asia. When the snows melt the waters descend southward along the course of the Mekong River and its tributaries, passing through China, Laos, Thailand, Cambodia and finally Vietnam. The silted channels of the Mekong River system are insufficient to accommodate the amount of water sent forth by the melting snows. The Mekong backs up and the impact of the overflow forces the Tonle Sap River to reverse its course each year between July and October and feed into the Great Lake. This action more than doubles the size of the lake, which normally covers an area of 3,000 square kilometres (1,158 square miles), and makes it a natural reservoir. When the waters from the snows drain off, the course of the Tonle Sap River reverses once again to resume its normal flow.

Zhou Daguan, a Chinese envoy of the Mongol Empire who lived at Angkor for a year in the late thirteenth century, gave the earliest recorded account of this feature:

> From the fourth to the ninth moon there is rain every afternoon, and the level of the Great Lake may rise seven to eight fathoms. Large trees go under water, with only the tops showing. People living at the water-side leave for the hills. However, from the tenth moon to the third moon of the following year not a drop of rain falls; the Great Lake is navigable only for the smallest craft, and the depth of the water is only three to five feet.[5]

The Great Lake was the lifeline of the Khmers. Its pattern of movement provided the rhythm of daily life and served as a source of fish and rice to an agrarian society. When the water doubled its volume the lake became an ideal feeding ground for spawning fish and, when it receded, the fish easily fell into the traps laid for them. This movement of the waters enabled the cultivation of floating rice, the earliest known form of Khmer agriculture. It is fast growing and germinates in deep water. The stems can grow up to 10 centimetres (4 inches) a day and reach a length of 6 metres (20 feet). The rice stays on the surface because its growth parallels the rise of the water level. Zhou Daguan recognized the unusual characteristics of floating rice and described 'a certain kind of land where the rice grows naturally, without sowing. When the water is up one fathom, the rice keeps pace in its growth. This, I think, must be a special variety', he noted 700 years ago.[6]

Historical Background

PREHISTORIC PERIOD

Evidence suggests that the early inhabitants of Cambodia lived at a similar time and at the same level of development as their neighbours in Burma, Laos, Thailand and Vietnam. The earliest habitation has been found in northwestern Cambodia at Loang Spean, which was occupied for some 5,000 years from the fourth millennium BC to the ninth century AD.[7] The people lived in caves and knew how to polish stone and decorate pottery with cord-marked, combed and carved designs. A second prehistoric site, Bas-Plateaux in southeastern Cambodia, was occupied from the second century BC to the eighth century AD.[8] The inhabitants of this later site lived in groups resembling villages. Their level of domestication was similar to that of the people of Loang Spean. Samrong Sen in central Cambodia, a third prehistoric site, was occupied about 1500 BC. The use of metal in Cambodia began about 1000 BC and became widespread by 500 BC. Human bones found in the area suggest a resemblance between the modern Cambodians and the people of the prehistoric period at Samrong Sen.[9]

It is generally agreed that the prehistoric period ended between 50 BC and AD 100 when Cambodia came into contact with China and India. The succeeding period, known as protohistoric, lasted until the ninth or tenth century. From then onwards sufficient historical records have survived to trace a continuous development of the people and places of Cambodia.

FIRST CENTURY TO EIGHTH CENTURY AD

The patterns of civilization established in prehistoric societies continued to develop in the protohistoric period. By the first century AD the coastal and valley regions comprised groups of settlements whose members cultivated rice, domesticated oxen, made low-fired earthenware for cooking food and storing liquids, and were adept at using metals. They practised animism, worshipping the spirits of the land and their ancestors.

During the early centuries of the Christian era the Chinese travelled by sea to the 'barbarian lands of the southern ocean' searching for new trade routes and commer-

---

5   Chou Ta-Kuan, *The Customs of Cambodia*, 2nd ed, Paul Pelliot, trans (The Siam Society, Bangkok, 1992), p 39.

6   Ibid.

7   J P Carbonnel, 'Recent Data on the Cambodian Neolithic: The Problem of Cultural Continuity in Southern Indochina', in *Early South East Asia, Essays in Archaeology, History and Historical Geography*, R B Smith and W Watson, eds (Oxford University Press, New York and Kuala Lumpur, 1979), pp 223–6.

8   Ibid, pp 224–5.

9   David P Chandler, *A History of Cambodia* (Westview Press, Boulder, Colorado, 1983), p 9.

cial outlets to replace the formerly lucrative overland passages to India which were blocked by nomadic tribes in Central Asia. Concurrently India ventured east for commercial purposes also, to establish trade with China by sea.

Initially ships followed the coastline, and mainland Southeast Asia rapidly emerged as a mid-way station along the route between China and India because of its position on the east–west axis and its protection by the inland sea. On the early route ships sailed from the eastern coast of India across the Bay of Bengal to the upper western coast of the Malay Peninsula. From there goods were transported by land across the Isthmus of Kra to the western coast of the Gulf of Thailand. Then they followed the coastline around the gulf and on to the southern provinces of China. Better knowledge of ship-building, improvements in navigational skills and the pattern of the monsoons accelerated the development of maritime trade between the two destinations by way of Southeast Asia.

Groups of settlers emerged at ports along the coast as use of the trade route increased. It seems likely that religious and social ideas from India reached the shores of Southeast Asia through these Indian-infiltrated areas and were transmitted by Brahman priests. Chinese records of the third century named Funan as an early Indianized state in mainland Southeast Asia. It was located in the area of the lower Mekong Delta of southeast Cambodia and south Vietnam. The inhabitants of this early state seem to have been a tribe of the Mon-Khmer group. Thus Funan was linked to Cambodia geographically and linguistically and as such is the earliest recorded predecessor of the Khmers. The name Funan may be a Chinese rendition of *bnam*, an ancient Khmer word meaning 'mountain' and sounding like *phnom* ('mountain' in modern Khmer).

Chinese texts record a legendary origin of Funan and later a variation of the same story was recounted in Sanskrit and Khmer inscriptions. A link between this legend and the origin of the Khmers and the lineage of the kings of Cambodia has persisted throughout history. There are many accounts of this story but one version is as follows. The race descended from the marriage of a foreigner to a local princess. One day the daughter of the king of the *nāgas*, the mythical serpents who inhabited the waters and ruled over the soil, saw a Hindu prince in a boat off the coast of Cambodia. She climbed into a small boat and rowed out to meet him. When he saw her he took his magical bow and shot an arrow into her boat. She was overcome by the action and married him. Her father gave the land of Cambodia and built a capital for his daughter's dowry. In another version of the story the prince hurled a javelin to mark the location of the capital. The name of the country was changed to Kambuja.

Indian ideas were absorbed into the culture of Funan during the early centuries of the Christian era on an increasing scale. A new influence seems to have arrived in the fifth century which may have been due to the presence of a Hindu ruler at Funan.

The main Indian concepts implanted in Southeast Asia during that time include the introduction of religions—both Hinduism and Buddhism—and the adoption of the Sanskrit language at court levels, which gave birth to a writing system and the first inscriptions. Other Indian ideas absorbed into the local culture were astronomy, a legal system, literature and universal kingship.

Civil wars undermined the stability of the state of Funan and by the early sixth century the centre of political power shifted inland. Chinese records suggest the emergence of a new state called Chenla (Zhenla) in the last half of the sixth century.

Zhenla seems to have gained control of Funan and expanded its territorial control over the next 200 years. Some time in the eighth century rivalry forced Zhenla to split into two parts, according to Chinese records. Upper Zhenla (of the Land), situated on the upper reaches of the Mekong in south Laos and along the northern shore of the Tonle Sap Lake, seems to correspond to the area of the original Zhenla. Throughout the eighth century it functioned as a centralized state with administrative centres at provincial capitals. Lower Zhenla (of the Water) was situated east of the Tonle Sap Lake with a capital at Īsānapura (Sambor Prei Kuk). It was less unified than the upper region and comprised several small states, including the former one of Funan in the Mekong Valley. The time from the fall of Funan to the beginning of the ninth century is known as the pre-Angkor Period of Cambodian history.

Western historians have long held the view that the states of Funan and Zhenla existed before the Khmer civilization. Knowledge of these states, though, relies solely on Chinese sources and their existence is not supported by either archaeological or epigraphical evidence. Additionally the names of the two states are not mentioned in any existing inscriptions of the time and they are unknown in the Khmer language. A more plausible theory, according to some scholars, is that Cambodia consisted of numerous states and that Funan and Zhenla were two of the most important ones. They may have called themselves kingdoms for the purpose of offering tribute to China.[10]

ANGKOR PERIOD (NINTH CENTURY TO FIFTEENTH CENTURY)

The generally accepted dates for the Angkor, or Kambuja, Period are 802 to 1432. During this time the Khmer Empire reached its greatest territorial limits and apogee in cultural and artistic achievements. The Angkor Period began when Jayavarman II declared himself king and ended when the Thais sacked the capital city of Angkor Thom. Dates of the Angkor Period were probably not definitive markers as the regions of the early capitals were inhabited both before and after.

---

[10] Claude Jacques, '"Funan", "Zhenla": The Reality Concealed by these Chinese Views of Indochina', in *Early South East Asia, Essays in Archaeology, History and Historical Geography*, R B Smith and W Watson, eds, pp 371–9.

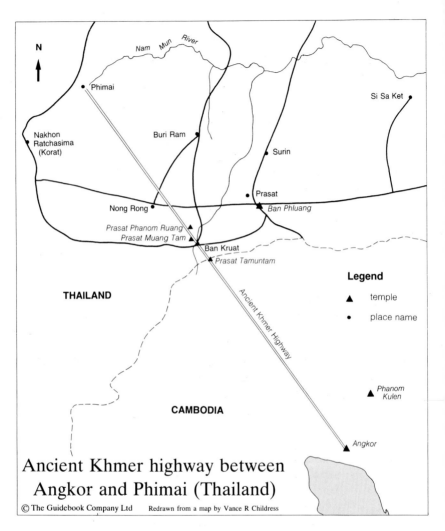

Ancient Khmer highway between Angkor and Phimai (Thailand)

© The Guidebook Company Ltd   Redrawn from a map by Vance R Childress

The history of this period has been reconstructed from the monuments and their reliefs, statuary, excavated artefacts and some 900 inscriptions in Pali, Sanskrit and Khmer—all found within the boundaries of the former empire. Inscriptions provide a genealogy and a chronological framework, describe the merits of the kings, and provide details about the temples such as the founding and inventories. Despite this seemingly large amount of evidence for the Ángkor Period, there are areas such as daily life where information is scarce.

The first appearance of the name Jayavarman was in the fifth century at the state of Funan where a king of that name ruled and sent diplomatic missions to China.

Jayavarman I reigned over Zhenla until his death in 681. Little is known about the reign of Jayavarman II as no inscriptions from his reign have been found. The reconstruction of the achievements of the first king of the Khmer Empire relies on the Sdok Kak Thom inscription dating from the middle of the eleventh century. It was found in northwestern Cambodia (and is now in the National Museum, Bangkok) and is the most important inscription, as regards historical content, on the reign of Jayavarman II. It says that Jayavarman spent some time at the court of the Śailendras dynasty in Indonesia before returning to Cambodia and proclaiming himself king. According to a later account by an Arab merchant, the King of the Śailendras dynasty staged a surprise attack on the Khmers by approaching the capital from the river and the Great Lake. The king was beheaded and the Khmer Empire became a vassal of the Śailendras dynasty.[11] Jayavarman may have been taken to Indonesia as a prisoner at the time of the attack.

He probably returned to Cambodia around 795 and soon after founded a capital at Indrapura. He then moved the capital three more times. The reasons for the changes are uncertain but it may have been for a better source of food. One of the locations of his capital was Hariharālaya (today Roluos). At the beginning of the ninth century Jayavarman II moved his capital again, this time to Mount Mahendrapura (today Phnom Kulen), 40 kilometres (25 miles) northeast of the city of Angkor Thom and proclaimed himself universal ruler. This historic event took place in 802 and marked the unification of the Khmer state, its independence from Indonesia, and the beginning of the Angkor Period. At the same time Jayavarman II installed the *devarāja* cult, a new religious belief. Soon afterwards he moved the capital back to Roluos where he ruled until his death in 850.

From this time onward a king inaugurated his reign and established his power by building a temple-mountain and installing the *devarāja* cult. A successful king ensured the prosperity of the kingdom and passed it on to his ancestors. His protective power was omnipotent and encompassed the people, state, law and soil. This factor was so important that the reign-names of successive kings included the honourary suffix -*varman* ('armour') which was later extended to mean 'protection' or 'protector'. In addition to a state temple a king sometimes built temples for his ancestors and a *baray* ('lake').

Women have held a position of respect and equality in Cambodian society throughout history. Inscriptions recount the hereditary lineage of the ruler often passing through a matriarchal line and the inheritance of property also being transmitted through the female line. Women figured in the government during the Angkor

---

[11] Lawrence Palmer Briggs, 'The Ancient Khmer Empire', idem, pp 67–8.

(following pages) *Early photograph of the ascent to the third level, Angkor Wat. The library is in the foreground, c. 1875*

Period and were also prominent in the economic structure of the Khmer Empire. Successive kings after Jayavarman II continued to unify and expand the Khmer Empire. A discussion of some of the more important ones follows. Indravarman I (reigned 877–89) built a large *baray* at Roluos to conserve water and constructed canals for irrigating rice fields in the area. Yaśovarman I (reigned 889–900) constructed a temple for his ancestors at Roluos and then moved the capital to Angkor which served as the Khmer centre for the next 500 years, except for a brief move to Koh Ker in the first half of the tenth century. He established his power at Phnom Bakheng, the first temple-mountain in the Angkor area, and built the East Baray for the storage of water.

Sūryavarman I (reigned 1002–50) brought peace and prosperity to the empire by strengthening the organization of the government and establishing internal security. He extended the territorial boundaries southward to the Gulf of Siam through a series of successful wars. His acquisitions included the region of Louvo (today Lopburi) which remained a Khmer centre for the next two centuries. His tolerant religious policy enabled both the *devarāja* cult and Buddhism to exist concurrently.

Sūryavarman II (reigned 1113–50) had a long reign in which he was besieged by invasions from neighbouring enemies—the Chams in south Vietnam and the Siamese (today Thais) in Thailand. Despite waging wars with these two kingdoms, he built Angkor Wat, the greatest architectural achievement of the Khmers.

Jayavarman VII (reigned 1181–1219) stands out today amongst the royal lineage because of his prolific construction of temples with immense appeal to foreigners. The Chams devastated the capital in 1177 in a surprise attack by approaching the region from the river and the Great Lake. Jayavarman VII drove out the Chams and restored order to the empire. He rebuilt the city of Angkor Thom and inaugurated Mahāyāna Buddhism, as manifested in the monument of the Bayon. The victories of the Khmers over the Chams in naval battles under the direction of Jayavarman VII are depicted on the historic reliefs of this temple. During his reign the boundaries of the empire extended from the coast of Vietnam to the borders of Pagan in Burma and from the vicinity of Vientiane in Laos to much of the Malay Peninsula. After his death Khmer power declined.

During the Angkor Period several kingdoms rose to power in the region and threatened the supremacy of the Khmer Empire. The names, dates and modern equivalents of the areas controlled by these kingdoms are summarized in the table opposite.

Champa was located in the Mekong Delta north of Funan in an area corresponding to central and south Vietnam. According to Chinese records, it was founded at the end of the second century. Indian influence penetrated Champa two or three hundred years later and Hinduism became the dominant religion. Linguistically the

Chams belong to the same group as the Indonesians. A link between the two cultures is seen in decorative motifs on Cham temples of the late ninth and early tenth centuries. Natural geographical barriers restricted the development of Champa into a centralized state. The Chams concentrated on maritime activities and became a strong naval power. After the collapse of Funan in the sixth century, the Chams extended their influence southward, but by the first half of the thirteenth century they came under the rule of the Khmers. Champa remained an independent state until the last half of the fifteenth century when it was absorbed by the Vietnamese.

The Mons established several centres in mainland Southeast Asia. The kingdom of Dvāravatī controlled the Menam Valley area from the sixth or seventh century to the eleventh century. The Pyus established a centre in the sixth century situated in the valleys of the central Irrawaddy and Sittang Rivers. Pegu, another Mon site, was founded in the ninth century. The Burmese emerged from the north in the eleventh century and took over the Pyus in the central valleys and established a capital at Pagan. The Burmese extended their territorial boundaries southward and conquered the Mons at Pegu.

Name	Period of Power (Centuries)	Area
Champa	2nd–15th	South Vietnam
Dvāravatī	6th/7th–11th	Thailand
Pyus	6th–11th	Burma
Śailendras	8th–9th	Indonesia (central Java)
Srivijaya	8th–13th	Indonesia (Sumatra); Malay
(9th–13th ruled by Śailendras)		Peninsula; South Thailand
Pegu	9th–11th	Burma
Pagan	11th–13th	Burma
Sukhothai	13th–14th	Thailand (north-central)
Lan Na	13th–16th	North Thailand
Ayutthaya	mid-14th–mid-18th	Thailand (central plain)

Two rival empires were situated in the Indonesian islands. The state of Srivijaya was founded in Sumatra at the end of the sixth century after Funan had been conquered, according to Chinese records. Its power extended to the coasts of West Java and Malaysia and to Chaiya in southern Thailand. The Srivijaya dynasty declined in the eleventh century because of a forced change in the trade routes brought about by increased piracy in the Sunda and Malacca Straits.

The Śailendras dynasty rose in Central Java in the eighth century and within a

(following pages) *Angkor and its environs, drawn by Lagrée and Garnier, 1873*

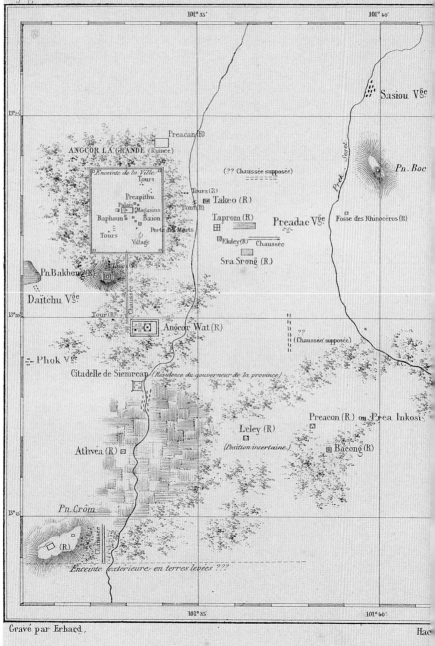

101° 35′   101° 40′

Sasiou Vᵍᵉ

13°25′

Preacan (R)

ANGCOR LA GRANDE (Ruinée)

Enceinte de la Ville
Tours

(?? Chaussée supposée)

Pᵘ. Boc

Tours (R)

Preapithu   Tours (R)
Palais   Magasins   Takeo (R)
Baphoun   Baion   Pont (R)

Taprom (R)   Preadac Vᵍᵉ   Fosse des Rhinocéros (R)

Tours   Porte des Morts
Village   Ekdey (R)   Chaussée

Sra Srong (R.)

Pⁿ. Bakheng (R)

Daïtchu Vᵍᵉ

13°20′

Tour (R)

Angcor Wat (R)

??
(Chaussée supposée)

Phok Vᵍᵉ

Citadelle de Siemreap (Résidence du gouverneur de la province)

Preacon (R) ou Prea Inkosi

Leley (R)
(Position incertaine.)

Bacong (R)

Athvéa (R)

13°15′

Pⁿ. Crôm

(R)   Chaussée

Enceinte extérieure en terres levées ???

101° 35′   101° 40′

Hac

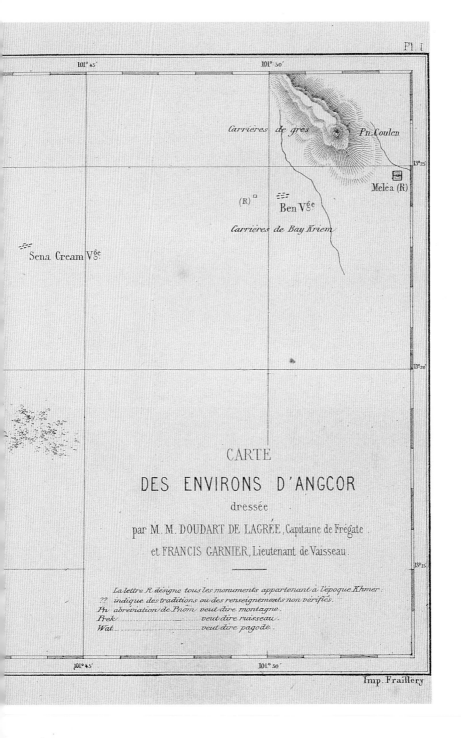

Pl. I

101° 45′   101° 50′

Carrières de grès   Pn. Coulen

13°25′

(R) □   Ben V.ᵍᵉ   Meléa (R)

Carrières de Bay Kriem

Sena Cream V.ᵍᵉ

13°20′

CARTE

DES ENVIRONS D'ANGCOR

dressée

par M. M. DOUDART DE LAGRÉE, Capitaine de Frégate

et FRANCIS GARNIER, Lieutenant de Vaisseau.

13°15′

La lettre R désigne tous les monuments appartenant à l'époque Khmer.
?? indique des traditions ou des renseignements non vérifiés.
Pn abreviation de Phom veut dire montagne.
Prek .... veut dire ruisseau.
Wat .... veut dire pagode.

101° 45′   101° 50′

Imp. Fraillery

hundred years gained control of Srivijaya. In the middle of the ninth century they constructed the Buddhist temple of Borobudur. Shortly afterwards the Śailendras lost control of Java but they reappeared on the throne of Srivijaya and remained in power until the thirteenth century.

Thailand was a persistent invader of Khmer territory. Sukhothai, the first organized settlement of the Thais, was centred in north-central Thailand and established in the thirteenth century. About the same time the Thai principality of Lan Na was founded with a capital at Chiang Mai. The Thais also controlled the area at the mouth of the Chao Phraya River which became the Ayutthaya kingdom in the middle of the fourteenth century. Within a hundred years the Thais had gained control of a large part of modern Thailand. Ayutthaya became the dominant power in the region until it was sacked by the Burmese in 1767. The Thais sacked Angkor in 1353 and even though the Khmers eventually recaptured it, battles between the two rivals continued for almost another century until 1431, when the Thais sacked the city of Angkor Thom.

The increasing strength of the Thais was a contributing factor to the decline of the territorial control of the Khmer Empire. Several other elements seem to have acted as catalysts for changes leading to the decline of the Khmer Empire. First, another form of Buddhism spread in the thirteenth century from Sri Lanka across mainland Southeast Asia from Burma to Thailand and on to Angkor and eclipsed the previous one. Theravāda Buddhism offered a new ideology that undermined the hold of Hinduism. Second, the people, perhaps buoyed by their new religious beliefs, revolted against conditions in the empire and its disintegrating internal structure. The loss of manpower through war and its effects meant that maintenance of the irrigation systems was neglected. The extensive building of monuments also depleted the resources of the empire. Third, as the central control weakened the vassal states asserted their independence and gradually became autonomous.

After the sacking of Angkor the capital was moved to Phnom Penh. The court returned to Angkor briefly in the late sixteenth century and again intermittently in the seventeenth century but it never regained its former glory. Other capitals were established at Lovek and Odong, both north of Phnom Penh.

THE REDISCOVERY OF ANGKOR

Henri Mouhot, a French naturalist, visited Cambodia in 1860 and is accredited with being the first foreigner to discover the ruins of Angkor after the capital was sacked by the Thais in the middle of the fifteenth century. Although Mouhot was the first European who was able to arouse interest in the ruins, the claim that he was the discoverer of Angkor is unfounded. Other foreigners saw and wrote about the site before he did, but their reports seem to have gone unnoticed by the West.

Numerous foreign traders from China, Japan, Arabia, Spain and Portugal resided in the Cambodian capitals of Phnom Penh and Lovek in the sixteenth century and they were joined briefly by the Dutch and the English in the following century. So it is not surprising that the ruins of Angkor were known to foreigners before Mouhot's visit. Portuguese refugees forced out of Sumatra by the Dutch in the sixteenth century sought asylum in Cambodia and were among the earliest Europeans to see Angkor. Other Portuguese and Spanish missionaries of the Franciscan and Dominican orders arrived from Malacca in the same century. Chronicles of the Portuguese compiled by Diogo do Couto contain several descriptions of Angkor. Although do Couto never visited Cambodia it is believed that Antonio de Magdalena, a Capuchin friar who visited Angkor about 1585, was his main source of information. He described a Cambodian king who went on an elephant hunt in the middle of the sixteenth century and came upon a 'number of imposing constructions' enshrouded in vegetation. He gave a detailed description of Angkor Wat and of the royal city of Angkor Thom.

Other early published reports seem to have been based on the same source as do Couto's account. Marcelo de Ribadeneira published a description of Angkor in 1601: 'There are in Cambodia the ruins of an ancient city, which some say was constructed by the Romans or by Alexander the Great.'[12] Gabriel Quiroga de San Antonio, a Spaniard, wrote in 1603: 'In 1570 a city was brought to light that had never been seen or heard of by the natives.'[13] Christoval de Jaque also reported visitors to the ruins in 1570 and in a book published on his travels in Indo-China in 1606 he called the site 'Anjog' and described the wall surrounding the city of Angkor Thom.[14] Spanish missionaries in Cambodia in the 1580s heard of a city of ancient ruins and prayed that the ruins 'may be rehabilitated to become an outpost of Christian missions outside the Philippines...'.[15] In 1672 Père Chevruel, a French missionary, wrote: 'There is an ancient and very celebrated temple situated at a distance of eight days from the place where I live. This temple is called Onco, and it is as famous among the gentiles as St Peter's at Rome.'[16] Few reports of Dutch visitors have come to light, which is surprising given their strong commercial presence in Southeast Asia in the sixteenth and seventeenth centuries. Gerard van Wusthoff wrote of Angkor in 1641 and 15 years later Hendrick Indjick wrote: 'The king paid a visit to a lovely pleasant place known

[12] Hugh Clifford, *Further India, Being the Story of Exploration from the Earliest Times in Burma, Malaya, Siam, and Indo-China* (Frederick A Stokes, New York, 1904, reprinted White Lotus, Bangkok, 1990), p 154.

[13] Donatella Mazzeo and Chiara Silvi Antonini, *Monuments of Civilization, Ancient Cambodia* (Grosset and Dunlap, New York, 1978), p 181.

[14] Ibid, p 154.

[15] Marcelo de Ribadeneira, *History of the Philippines and Other Kingdoms*, 17, Vol 1, Pt 2, Pacita Guevara Fernandez, trans (The Historical Conservation Society, Manila, 1970), p 441.

[16] Ibid, p 154.

as Anckoor, which the Portuguese and Castilians call Rome, and which is situated an eight- or ten-day journey from here [Phnom Penh].'[17]

Evidence of the Japanese at Angkor in the seventeenth century is carved in sandstone at Angkor Wat. Calligraphic characters corresponding to the date of 1632 can be seen on a pillar of the second level of Angkor Wat. They were purportedly written by Morimoto Ukondayu who visited Angkor in that year and reportedly dedicated four Buddha images to Angkor Wat in honour of his father. Kenryo Shimano, a Japanese interpreter from Nagasaki, went to Angkor some time between 1632 and 1636 and drew a remarkably accurate diagram of the temple that is the oldest known plan of Angkor Wat. Even though he called it Jetavana-vihāra, a Buddhist site in India, and Angkor is not named on the diagram, other facts such as the unusual layout and orientation to the west confirm the identity of Angkor Wat. The most remarkable reference is a note on the diagram that says 'sculptures in relief ... four gods pull the rope', which clearly refers to the Churning of the Ocean of Milk in the gallery of bas-reliefs at Angkor Wat.

Other foreigners published unrecognized accounts. Dr House, an American missionary and long-time resident of Siam, wrote a lively and interesting description of Angkor in 1855, five years before Henri Mouhot visited the ruins. Like others, this account never seemed to reach the ear or the eye of the public. Charles-Emile Bouille-vaux, a French missionary, saw Angkor in 1850 and published an account of his travels eight years later, but it too never attracted public attention. D O King, an Englishman in Siam and Cambodia in 1859—a year before Mouhot—read a paper to the Royal Geographical Society in London in the same year. He noted the following points about the ruins: the existence of a map in a French work, the notice of a large lake, and the ruins. 'The Temple stands solitary and alone in the jungle, in too perfect order to be called a ruin, a relic of a race far ahead of the present in all the arts and sciences', he wrote.[18] It is not clear why his paper went unrecognized but by then Mouhot had left England for Southeast Asia.

Although Mouhot was French, his wife was English and they lived in England. Inspired by a book on Siam loaned to him by a friend, he organized a trip to the East and was fortunate to gain the support of the Royal Geographical Society of London although he received no financial assistance. Mouhot departed for the East in 1858 and travelled overland in Siam and Cambodia. He surveyed and measured the temple of Angkor Wat and kept detailed notes on his observations of the ruins. In 1861 Mouhot contracted a fever and died in Laos at the age of 35. His diaries and extracts from his travel correspondence were published posthumously in 1864.

---

[17]   Ibid, p 183.
[18]   D O King, 'Travels in Siam and Cambodia', *Journal of the Royal Geographical Society*, Vol 30, 1860, pp 177–82.

Pilgrimage to Angkor

Frank Vincent, Jr, a frail young American who dropped out of university because of illness at the age of seventeen, was determined '...to make a systematic tour of the most interesting parts of the world'. In 1872, he visited Cambodia and the ancient ruins of Angkor. Vincent describes his journey overland from Bangkok to Siem Reap, the village closest to the ruins, in vivid detail. 'The total distance we travelled from Bangkok was 175 miles; of this 30 miles was by canal in boats, 30 miles on the Bang pa Kong river in boats, and the remainder—215 miles—was performed upon horses and elephants, in bullock-carts, and on foot; the greater part of the journey, however, was accomplished on horseback. The time consumed in making this trip was seventeen days.

'The governor of Siamrap having provided us with three elephants, on the 13th inst, we started for the ruins of Angkor, three and a half miles distant, to the north. We took but little baggage with us, being rather impatient now that we were nearing the main object of the expedition—the ultima Thule of our desires and hopes—and so we passed quickly and silently along a narrow but good road cut through the dense, riant forest, until, in about an hour's time, on suddenly emerging from the woods, we saw a little way off to the right, across a pond filled with lotus plants, a long row of columned galleries, and beyond—high above the beautiful cocoa and areca palms—three or four immense pagodas, built of a dark-grey stone. And my heart almost bounded into my mouth as the Cambodian driver, turning towards the howday, said, with a bright flash of the eye and a proud turn of the lip, "Naghon Wat"; for we were then at the very portals of the famous old "City of Monasteries", and not far distant was Angkorthom—Angkor the Great.'

Frank Vincent, Jr, The Land of the White Elephant:
Sights and Scenes in Southeast Asia 1871–1872
(Oxford University Press, rep, Singapore, 1988)

COMMISSION D'

M. GARNIER.   M. DELAPORTE.   M. JOUBERT.

M. THOREL.   M. DE CARNÉ   M. DE LAGRÉE.

John Thomson, an Englishman and a renowned photographer, published the first photographic account of the ruins in 1875 and included a description of the bas-reliefs at Angkor Wat and a plan (to scale) of the temple based on his own survey.[19] 'I can hardly conceive of anything more startling than the first sight of this great temple, after a month's journey through the forests and jungles of Siam', he wrote.[20]

By the time Mouhot's diaries were published France had a presence in Indo-China. By 1863 a French Protectorate over Cambodia was in place except for Battambang and Siem Reap provinces, which were under the jurisdiction of Siam. A treaty between Thailand and France in 1907 ceded these territories to France. An unsettled aftermath of this treaty was that there was a small area of land on the eastern side of the Dangrek Mountains where the temple of Khao Prah Viharn was located and over which both Cambodia and Thailand claimed territorial rights. The dispute was settled by the International Court of Justice in 1962, which awarded the area to Cambodia. The temple, however, is situated at the apex of a 600-metre (1,968-foot) cliff and the only feasible access to it is from Thailand. The temple of Banteay Srei, northeast of Angkor, was another site of dispute because it was located in the territory granted to Thailand. In 1941 the Japanese served as mediators in negotiations between Thailand and France and it was decided the temple should belong to Cambodia.

In 1866 Doudart de Lagrée, organizer of the French Protectorate, inspected the ruins at Angkor. Several members of his group, such as Francis Garnier and Louis Delaporte, became pioneers in the exploration of Angkor. Delaporte conducted a survey of Angkor in 1871 and published his findings and drawings in *Voyage au Cambodge* (Paris, 1880)—four of which are reproduced in this guidebook. Lunet de Lajonquière published the first complete plans of the ruins in 1900.[21]

In 1898 the French founded the École Française d'Extrême Orient (French School of the Far East) to study the history, language and archaeology of Far Eastern countries. The goals for Cambodia were to make scientific explorations of the ruins and to take measures to preserve them. The Angkor Conservancy at Siem Reap was set up in the same year. Except during the Second World War, the French worked at Angkor continuously until 1972 when they were forced to leave because of civil war.

The dedication of the French is noteworthy. Among those working in the first two decades of this century were Jean Commaille, first conservator of the monuments at Angkor, Henri Parmentier, chief of the archaeological services of French Indo-

---

[19] John Thomson, *The Straits of Malacca, Siam and Indo-China or Ten Years' Travels, Adventures and Residence Abroad* (Sampson Low, Marston, Low and Searle, London, 1875, rep Oxford University Press, Singapore, 1993).

[20] John Thomson, 'Notes of a Journey through Siam to the Ruin of Cambodia Communicated to the Royal Geographical Society' [Unpublished Manuscript], *Journal Southeast Asia*, 1866, p 199.

[21] Lunet de Lajonquière, *Inventaire descriptif des monuments du Cambodge* (École Française d'Extrême Orient, Paris, 1902–11) Vols IV, VIII and IX.

Female divinities in niches at Banteay Kdei

China, and Henri Marchal. Some archaeologists spent their lives in Cambodia. The Groslier family, for example, left a legacy started by Georges in the 1920s and continued by his son, Bernard-Philippe, who was the last of the French to leave Cambodia in 1972. Some 900 inscriptions were translated by the French and provide a definitive source for dating. George Cœdès was one of the leading French scholars on Khmer art and history. Philippe Stern traced the evolution of the art of Angkor and Pierre Dupont established the pre-Angkor history. The restoration of the monuments took place mainly from 1933 onwards under the guidance of George Trouvé and Maurice Glaize. After France officially handed over Cambodia in 1953 French archaeologists were invited to continue their work on the monuments under the terms of a 'freely negotiated agreement'.

MODERN DEVELOPMENTS AT ANGKOR

Damage to the monuments from warfare since 1972 was minimal, contrary to rumours and erroneous press reports. Other than a few scars from bullets and shrapnel at the entrance and along the west wall there is little evidence of war at Angkor Wat. The monuments of Angkor are, however, threatened by the rapid growth of tropical forests, monsoonal rainfall and theft.

The jungle is eating away at the monuments. Lichens, minuscule plants that look like a multi-coloured crust clinging to the trunks of stone, are amongst the worst enemies and need to be eradicated. Two other culprits of nature are the kapok or silk-cotton tree, which is distinguished by its straight trunk, buff-coloured bark and branches spreading at right angles that look like the spokes of an umbrella; and the fig tree, with its gigantic coiling roots and a trunk that looks like several joined together.

Archaeological evidence shows a vast network of water facilities in the area of Angkor and some scholars believe that the presence of these enormous reservoirs, dykes and canals meant that the Khmers had knowledge of advanced irrigation techniques. A recent theory has challenged the idea that the Khmers were capable of irrigation and flood control on a large scale. Engineers, using remote sensing equipment and satellite images to study the land formations, have been able to determine how the Khmers grew and irrigated their crops. The study found little evidence of the existence of an extensive irrigation system. They suggest the large moats surrounding many of the monuments at Angkor could not have been used to irrigate crops, as previously believed, because there are no outlets from these moats into the fields.[22]

According to the same research source, the soil in the Angkor region was not fertile enough for the cultivation of several crops of rice a year to sustain the work force required for the extensive building programmes of the Khmers, as was previously believed. Tests conducted by foreign engineers revealed a coarse sandy soil and erosion caused by rainfall and melting snows. The study concluded that the soil would not have been adequate to support the cultivation of many crops annually over a long period.[23]

The fluctuating water table underneath the monuments threatens their structural stability, which was secure only as long as the water table remained constant. Clogged moats and connecting channels prevent the drainage of excess water. In the past, rain falling on the stone monuments filtered down to the laterite foundations and then into moats, canals and irrigation channels. Without drainage, the monuments are standing in water that seeps into the sandstone and causes mould. This environment contributes to the destruction of the carvings and the solidity of the structure as a whole.

The theft of artefacts at Angkor is reportedly an organized trade on a large scale and poses a serious threat to the heritage of the Khmer civilization. Improved border relations between Thailand and Cambodia facilitate the smuggling of art across the border. From there the art pieces are taken to Bangkok and later sold in the international market. The Angkor Conservancy at Siem Reap is replacing original heads at the entrances at Angkor Thom with replicas in an effort to preserve the art. The originals are held at the Angkor Conservancy. There is a need for guards, legislation and security systems for the protection of the monuments in Cambodia.

The monuments at Angkor are currently under the jurisdiction of the United Nations Educational, Scientific and Cultural Organization (UNESCO), which acts as coordinator and international non-partisan body. It aims to put together a programme of technical and financial assistance for saving the monuments. The plan includes a programme to train Cambodians in the fields of archaeology and conservation. Only three trained Cambodian archaeologists survived the Pol Pot regime and only two of 1,000 workers employed by the French survived. The Fine Arts Department of the University of Phnom Penh re-opened in 1989 and is dedicated to training in the fields necessary for the preservation of the Cambodian monuments.

[22] Gary van Zuylen, 'The flow of history, Did Khmer riches come from irrigation?', *The Nation*, Bangkok, 17 September 1991.
[23] W J Van Liere, 'Traditional Water Management in the Lower Mekong Basin', *World Archaeology*, Vol 11, No 3, 1980, pp 265–80.

Religion

As the principles of religion governed the concept and execution of all Khmer art and architecture, an appreciation of Angkor and its civilization is enhanced by an understanding of the religious beliefs of the Khmers.

ANIMISM

The earliest form of worship in Cambodia was a widespread primitive belief in animism or spiritual forces. Patronage to it continued even after the adoption of religious practices from India in the early centuries of the Christian era. The presence of spirits in all material things—trees, rivers, mountains, stones and the earth—exerted a profound influence on daily life. Supernatural forces were both revered and feared and, because of this duality, widespread superstitions surrounded them. They had to be either invoked or appeased through rituals. People gave special attention to the spirits of water, because of its necessity for man's survival. The spirits of ancestors also required nurturing and pacifying because, according to belief, when a person died his soul was reincarnated and his spirit became a free agent.

The formal religious practices adopted in Cambodia at a later date recognized a common belief in rebirth or the idea that one is born again and again in different forms. The ultimate goal is release from the chain of rebirth.

BRAHMANISM

This religion was brought to India by the Aryans. The principles of this religion developed from about 900 to 550 BC and were reflected in hymns known as the Vedas. Gods stemming from the Vedic beliefs that are depicted in Khmer art include Agni, Indra and Sūrya. Followers of Brahmanism worshipped images, recognized the forces of animistic spirits, and believed in the endless cycle of creation and destruction. Brahmanism adopted the ancient concept of the cosmology of the world with a mountain called Meru situated at the axis of the universe.

HINDUISM

The fusion of Brahmanism and early beliefs of the Vedic traditions gave birth to Hinduism. Its concepts were probably formulated at the beginning of the Christian era. Hinduism is the dominant religion in India today. Followers believe in a universal world spirit called Brahmanism and worship, among others, the deities of the Trinity—Brahmā, Śiva and Viṣṇu. Each of these gods inspired a religious cult that became an important form of worship at Angkor. Śivaism was the earliest and one of the most important cults in Cambodia. In the eleventh century it was supplanted by Viṣṇuism.

Bas-relief of the image of the Hindu god Viṣṇu carrying his attributes and standing on the shoulders of Garuḍa, Prasat Kravan

DEVARĀJA

A cult associated with the rulers of Angkor was the *devarāja*, meaning either 'god-king' or 'king of the gods'. Opinions differ on the interpretation of this Sanskrit word but it is generally agreed that the Khmer king was considered an earthly representation of a deity. The king was imbued with divine direction and power through a consecration rite of the *devarāja* and as such was responsible for the security and welfare of the state. The ruler's role is reflected in the translation of the Khmer name of the cult 'the Lord of the Universe who is King', which appears in inscriptions. Research based on epigraphic sources argues, though, that there is no evidence of the ruler's consecration as god-king.[24] The cult was installed as the official religion in Cambodia in 802 by Jayavarman II. It subsequently became synonymous with royalty and provided a symbolical vehicle unifying the Khmer Empire and enabling a ruler to establish himself and his reign.

A king identified with a personal deity of his choice. The earliest representation of

[24] Herman Kulke, *The Devarāja Cult*, trans by I W Mabbett and J M Jacob, Ithaca, New York, Data Paper: Number 108, Southeast Asia Program, Department of Asian Studies, Cornell University, January 1978.

the *devarāja* cult was a *liṅga* installed at a rite in the sacred sanctuary of a temple-mountain and adhered to by a ruler worshipping Śiva. Later the cult was fostered by worshippers of Viṣṇu or the Buddha and appropriate symbols were installed. A *liṅga* ('sign') symbolizes the creative energy of the powers of nature. A typical *liṅga* is shaped like an erect phallus and usually made of polished stone. The vertical shaft is sometimes divided into three parts symbolizing the Trinity. The lower, square portion represents Brahmā. An octagonal section in the middle relates to Viṣṇu. The upper, cylindrical part with a rounded tip is associated with Śiva. The base of the *liṅga* is anchored at the centre of a square pedestal which has a hollow channel on one side for the waters of ablution to flow out.

BUDDHISM

This religion began in India as a reform movement against Hinduism. By the second century of the Christian era two strains of Buddhism were defined—Mahāyāna and Theravāda. Both of these were transmitted to Cambodia. Mahāyāna Buddhism, known as the Greater Vehicle, may have reached Cambodia by way of the Kingdom of Srivijaya (Indonesia) and Funan where it was practised in the fifth century. Although Mahāyāna Buddhism had some following during the early Angkor Period, it reached a peak of dominance in the late twelfth and thirteenth centuries during the reign of Jayavarman VII. It is practised today in Nepal, Tibet, Bhutan, Mongolia, China, Korea, Japan and North Vietnam. Followers of Mahāyāna Buddhism believe in the attainment of buddhahood and the removal of all ignorance. The principles of this sect are expounded through the Sanskrit language.

The Theravāda strain spread gradually from Sri Lanka to mainland Southeast Asia by way of Burma and Thailand between the eleventh and fifteenth centuries and is practised in those areas today. Theravāda Buddhism, known as the Lesser Vehicle, adhered to conservative principles preserving the original doctrines and expressed them through the Pali language.

By the seventh century tenets from animism, Brahmanism, Hinduism, Buddhism and related cults were synthesized to suit the ideological and aesthetic ideals of the inhabitants of the mainland. The coexistence of these different principles was a unique aspect of religious practice in Cambodia. One belief or another always dominated but the supremacy varied and it was rarely at the exclusion of others. Buddhism, for example, was influenced by Hindu cult practices and also absorbed images of animistic spirits into its doctrines. While Buddhism rejected some of the doctrines of Brahmanism it borrowed a few of the Hindu deities. Likewise Hinduism embraced gods from the ancient traditions along with those of the Trinity. Khmer art also reflects this amalgamation of beliefs. Some legends depicted on the reliefs, for example, incorporate aspects of both Hinduism and Buddhism. And the god Hari-Hara, popular in early Khmer art, is a composite figure with features of two forms of cult worships —Śivaism and Viṣṇuism.

HINDU DEITIES

The Hindu pantheon of gods and goddesses is a vast and complex one. Knowing a few characteristics of the major deities can help in identifying them and enhance one's appreciation of Angkor. Khmer deities are eternally youthful, yet have a noble air of elegance. They appear sitting, standing or reclining, without eroticism or nakedness. Their faces show no emotion except for a serene expression. Identification, therefore, is not revealed in the face but in other features. The presence of a wife or consort of a god who represents his female energy or *śaktī* can sometimes help to identify the god. The objects or weapons, known as attributes, that a god holds in his hands and the animal he rides are other distinguishing features.

Some of the main objects held by deities and their characteristics in Khmer art follow. A **club**, or **mace**, is represented as a weapon with a tapered top and a bulbous lower section. It was used for close combat. A **conch**, in its form as an attribute of a god, emulates a natural conch shell. A **disc**, or *cakra*, looks like a miniature wheel with spokes and is often elaborately decorated. It represents power and the rotation of the world; and, in Buddhism, the Wheel of Law. An **elephant goad** is depicted as a stick with a small handle and a sharp hook. A fly whisk looks like a shaft with pointed tufts of hair. A so-called rosary used by both Hindu and Buddhist deities is a string of beads. A trident is an indestructible weapon that represents absolute truth and has the power to destroy everything evil. It looks like a large three-pronged fork with a long handle. A double trident is sometimes called a thunderbolt. A vase with a round body and flaring mouth symbolizes a container filled with the Water of Life.

A description of the main divinities and other mythical beings, along with their attributes and symbolical characteristics, follows. These are, however, only guidelines and none of the deities has only the features mentioned all the time. They define a particular form depicted in Khmer art but when the deity appears in another manifestation or time, the symbolism changes (for a summary of the deities and their characteristics see Appendix V, page 225).

Agni (God of Fire) lives on earth and serves as a mediator between men and gods. *Characteristics*: four arms, two heads which symbolize the sacrificial fire and the fire of the domestic hearth; he holds a fan to put out the fire, an axe, a torch and a ladle; his mount is a rhinoceros.

Brahmā (The Creator) According to legend, Brahmā was born from a golden lotus that emerged from the navel of Viṣṇu, who was reclining on a serpent on the waves of the ocean during a cosmic sleep. Characteristics: four faces symbolizing his domination over all regions of space; among the objects he frequently carries are a disc, a ladle, a book, a rosary, a vase, a fly whisk and sceptre; his mount is the *haṃsa*, a sacred goose; his wife is Sarasvatī, the Goddess of Knowledge.

Durgā One of the wives of Śiva. Daughter of the mountain god of a fierce aspect. In this form she rides a tiger and fights a buffalo.

Gaṇeśa (God of Wisdom) is the son of Śiva and Pārvatī. Depictions of Gaṇeśa on reliefs at Angkor are uncommon but he was a popular deity and is usually seen in sculpted form. Gaṇeśa was probably originally a god of fertility. Tales of his birth vary but according to one legend Gaṇeśa was born with a human head. Appointed to guard Pārvatī's door and to refuse entry to anyone, he forbade Śiva to enter. Angry that he could not enter his wife's quarters, Śiva beheaded his son. Pārvatī pleaded with Śiva to save Gaṇeśa's life. So Śiva gave him the head of the next creature he encountered, which happened to be an elephant. *Characteristics*: he has a corpulent body in the shape of a human with the head of an elephant; he sometimes sits with his trunk in a bowl resting in one of his hands; he has either two or four arms and carries an elephant goad and a noose; Gaṇeśa has only one tusk and holds the other in his hand. He rides a rat.

Ganga The second wife of Śiva. According to legend, Ganga, a river goddess, descended from heaven and was caught by Śiva in his hair to spare the earth the shock of her fall.

Hari-Hara combines aspects of Viṣṇu (Hari) on one side, and Śiva (Hara), on the other side, into one deity. *Characteristics*: his headdress has the tiara of Viṣṇu and the plaited locks of Śiva's ascetic form; he holds the objects of each of the gods he represents.

Indra (God of the Sky) is the king of the gods and ruler of the world and space. He lives in a palace of gold at the summit of Mount Meru in paradise. *Characteristics*: he wears a high tiara or turban and is dressed in elaborate clothes and jewellery; he holds a thunderbolt as his main weapon and also carries a disc, an elephant goad, and an axe to make rivers flow; he rides a white elephant which often has three heads and is known as Airāvata.

Kāma (God of Love) *Characteristics*: carries a bow adorned with flowers and a case of floral arrows made of a lotus, a lily, mace, jasmine, and gold flowers from the mango tree; usually has two or eight arms; his mount is a parrot and his wife is Rati.

Kubera (God of Wealth) is Guardian of the North and chief of the *yakṣas*. *Characteristics*: he is a fat dwarf; he wears a crown and jewellery; Kubera usually carries a lemon or a pomegranate in one hand and a mongoose spitting jewels in the other; money bags symbolizing wealth are often found near him; he rides a horse.

Lakṣmī (Goddess of Beauty) was born of the Churning of the Ocean of Milk and is the wife of Viṣṇu. She is also known as Śrī, the Goddess of Good Fortune. Lakṣmī descended to earth as one of his *avatāras*. She is often depicted in Khmer art as Sītā,

Triangular-shaped pediments framed with elaborately decorated scrolls, 12th century

48

the wife of Rāma. *Characteristics*: she usually has two but sometimes four arms; is often depicted on a lotus pedestal holding a lotus blossom and the conch, disc and club of Viṣṇu; she is sometimes attended by two elephants who sprinkle lustral water on her with raised trunks.

Pārvatī ('daughter of the mountain') is the chief wife of Śiva. She has many forms and is sometimes called Umā. As her fierce aspect she is Durgā. *Characteristics*: she wears a chignon with curls, has either two or four arms and holds a lotus, a rosary, a vase, and sometimes the trident of Śiva; she is often on a lotus pedestal. Her mount is a lion.

Rati One of the wives of Kāma. Goddess of 'love, desire, sexual lust or union'.

Sarasvatī (Goddess of Eloquence) Wife of Brahmā. *Characteristics*: she holds a flute and a book. Her mount is a peacock.

Śiva (The Destroyer) In the art of pre-Angkor he was part of the composite figure Hari-Hara and was later represented in the form of a *liṅga*. Although Śiva is the destroyer he is also closely connected with his auspicious aspect. Śiva is the originator of all performing arts and through the rhythm of his dancing he regulates the destiny of the world. He lives on Mount Meru. *Characteristics*: he wears a chignon with curls and has a third eye in the middle of his forehead near his brow (this eye is in a vertical position and it is always closed because, according to legend, if it opens the whole universe will be destroyed by a great fire). He usually has four arms. The objects he holds vary according to his forms but the most common one is a trident; sometimes Śiva is depicted as an ascetic with a bare torso wrapped with a Brahmānic cord that often emulates a serpent; his wife is Pārvatī. He rides the bull, Nandi, who is as 'white as the Himalayan peaks'. In Khmer art Śiva and Pārvatī are sometimes seated on the bull and, at other times, he holds his wife on his knee. They have two sons—Skanda, the God of War, and Gaṇeśa, the God of Knowledge.

Skanda (God of War) is the son of Śiva and Pārvatī. *Characteristics*: he either wears a tiara or has his hair divided into three locks and knotted on top of his head; he often has six heads and arms; he carries a double thunderbolt, a sword and a trident; his mount is a peacock; at the Gallery of Bas-reliefs at Angkor Wat, Skanda is depicted as an archer with an arrow made by Sūrya, God of the Sun, from the heat and energy of the sun.

Śrī (Goddess of Good Fortune) Also known as Lakṣmī.

Sūrya (God of the Sun) *Characteristics*: he wears a long tunic and high boots and often appears with another cosmic symbol, the moon; he sometimes holds a lotus and rides in a chariot drawn by seven horses.

Umā ('the gracious one') Wife of Śiva.

Viṣṇu (The Preserver) Viṣṇu is the preserver in the Trinity and inspired a cult that was popular in Cambodia during the eleventh and twelfth centuries. He is usually depicted as a young man with perfect proportions. *Characteristics*: he wears a *sampot* with a belt and a cylindrical headdress in pre-Angkor art and later in the Angkor Period he wears a diadem; he has four arms and holds a conch, a disc, a club and a ball or a lotus; Viṣṇu rides a Garuḍa, the mythical king of birds with a human body; his wife is Lakṣmī.

Whenever the world is threatened by evil, Viṣṇu assumes the role of saviour and descends to earth in a suitable form. He is reincarnated as a human or animal and triumphs over the forces of evil. The most common *avatāras* or incarnations of Viṣṇu are: (1) a **Fish** with a human torso who saved the founder of present-day humanity; (2) a **Tortoise** with a human torso, who serves as the base of the mountain and supports the universe in the episode of the Churning of the Ocean of Milk; (3) a **Boar** with the body of a man who holds the goddess Earth in his arms (uncommon); (4) a **Man-lion** who attacks the king of the demons with his paws; (5) a **Dwarf** who obtains the earth, sky and hell in three strides to assure the gods possession of the world; (6) **Rāma** in human form with an axe; (7) **Rāma** the hero of the *Rāmāyana*; (8) **Kṛṣṇa**; (9) **Buddha**; and (10) a **Man-horse**.

Yama (God of Justice and the Underworld) He is also known as the Lord of Law and Supreme Judge. Yama allots seats after death in heaven or hell in accordance with an individual's performance in the world. *Characteristics*: Yama has multiple arms (usually eight) and holds the weapons of justice (clubs) necessary for judging the dead and determining their fate; his mount is a buffalo.

HINDU MYTHICAL BEINGS

Besides deities, there are numerous minor divinities and mythical beings depicted in Khmer art. Some of those most frequently shown are:

Ananta ('endless') The snake upon which Śiva rests when he is in a cosmic sleep.

apsarā (female minor divinity) A celestial nymph, a dancer and a courtesan of the sky. An *apsarā* has perfect beauty and evokes irresistible seduction. The ultimate depiction of the *apsarā* appears in the bas-reliefs on the walls of the third gallery at Angkor Wat.

asura (demon) An *asura* represents the forces of darkness or evil and is the enemy of the gods.

Bali A demon king who was dethroned from his domination over the world by Viṣṇu.

Bana (demon) *Characteristics*: he has multiple arms and rides in a chariot drawn by lions.

dvārapāla (Guardian of the Gate) This large figure is also known as the protector of shrines. *Characteristics*: often standing at the entrance to temples; carries a club.

Garuḍa is the mount of Viṣṇu and the enemy of the *nāgas*. He appears on the

A pair of heavenly dancers on the interior of the second level gallery, Angkor Wat

[Garuḍa] In his heavy shape we must not look for lightness only and delicacy...his is the strength of the great element, marvellous, but not always innocent. He possesses the head of vultures, with the eyes reputed to be the acutest in nature, and with the power of smell which is able to notice, in spite of wide distances, the odour of carrion; he has also wings of the same rapacious bird of prey unmatched by any others; in the lofty regions of the clouds he glides, and remains suspended to the stars by a thin thread, which allows him never to retire, to reign where all is vapour, and trace vast circles in emptiness. His arms and hands are those of men...and they are shown there to personify the power of air to strike or caress, to sing or murmur, to hold or to liberate. Finally his body and legs are those of tigers: suppleness incarnate, grace in flesh, and crushing power turned into limbs, abdomen and breast. They are the velocity of the wind, the sudden leap of storms and the grace of clouds.

P J de Beerski, Angkor: Ruins in Cambodia *(Houghton Mifflin, London, Boston & New York, 1924)*

walls enclosing temples with arms stretched above his head and grasping the tails of serpents whose heads curl up at its feet. *Characteristics*: a gigantic mythical bird with a human body and wings, legs and a thick curved bird-like beak with bulging eyes; the lower part of his body is covered with feathers and he has the claws of an eagle; he wears a diadem and jewellery.

kāla is a mask-like creature commonly found in both Hindu and Buddhist temples. It serves as a protector for the temples and as such is found above the doorways. According to legend, the *kāla* had a voracious appetite and asked Śiva for a victim to satiate itself. Śiva was angered by the request and ordered the *kāla* to devour itself. *Kāla* consumed its body but not its head. When Śiva heard that the *kāla* had followed his order he had its head placed over the doors of temples as a reminder of his 'terrible and beneficent' powers. *Characteristics*: round bulbous eyes, a human or lion's nose, grinning, two horns and claw-like hands.

Kṛṣṇa is a hero in the epic *Mahābhārata* and is one of the *avatāras* of Viṣṇu. He appeared on earth to save mankind from the tyranny of the demon king. He is often depicted as a baby or a young shepherd.

lokapāla ('world protector') A protector of one of the eight directions of the earth in Hindu mythology; also figures in the legends of the life of the Buddha.

makara Characteristics: a large sea animal with the body of a reptile and a big jaw and snout that is elongated into a trunk; often depicted spewing another creature or plant motif from its mouth.

nāga ('snake') A semi-divine being and a serpent-god of the waters who lives in the underworld beneath the earth or in the water. The *nāgas* are ruled by Vāsuki and are the enemy of the Garuḍa. The *nāga* controls the prosperity of the region where it resides and the rains. *Nāgas* commonly marry humans in mythology and the Khmers claim their descent from the union of a foreigner and the daughter of the *nāga* king. The Khmers' obsession with the *nāga* is reflected in its omnipresence at the temples of Angkor. It is seemingly everywhere. A typical rendering of this mythical being is a balustrade formed by the body of the serpent. Such balustrades flank the long causeways leading to the monuments. *Characteristics*: usually depicted with the scaly body of a serpent and multiple heads spread in the shape of a fan.

Nandi (bull) The mount of Śiva.

Rāhu (demon) *Characteristics*: he is similar to a *kāla* as he has no body but he has hands and is often holding a moon in his mouth. According to legend, the moon contains the elixir of immortality and when he catches it he swallows the moon and causes an eclipse. The moon reappears through the throat of Rāhu and ends the eclipse so Rāhu must resume the chase.

Vāsuki The serpent who served as a rope when the Ocean of Milk was churned by the gods and demons. He is sometimes called Śeṣa or Ananta.

yakṣa A semi-divine being who has both a good and an evil form. In Khmer art a *yakṣa* is usually a demon. In the *Rāmāyana* this figure is a demon giant who lives on the island of Laṅkā. A *yakṣa* can change its shape and fly. *Characteristics*: large size, bulging eyes, fangs, a leering grin.

Legends Depicted in Khmer Art

The narrative scenes depicted in Khmer art are inspired by Hindu and Buddhist iconography. The Hindu myths draw from the great Indian epics, among them the *Rāmāyana* and the *Mahābhārata*. Summaries of some of the legends that inspired artistic renditions on the reliefs of the monuments of Angkor follow.

■ HINDU LEGENDS
RĀMĀYANA

The Hindu epic the *Rāmāyana* (*Reamker* is the Cambodian version) has penetrated the art and culture of all South and Southeast Asian countries. It is generally accepted that its composition took place between 200 BC and AD 200. The early date, long evolution, wide distribution and complexities in translations have resulted in numerous changes, additions and variations. Thus the legacy of the *Rāmāyana* consists of many versions and sources differ. A summary of a standard version of the epic that includes scenes and characters depicted in Khmer art of the Angkor Period follows. The characters in this version of the *Rāmāyana* are:

Hanumān: monkey-headed demi-god
Indrajit: 'the invisible warrior'; son of Rāvana
King of Ayodhya: stepfather of Rāma
Lakṣmana: brother of Rāma
Marica: a demon disguised as a golden stag
rākṣasa: 'night wanderer'; a demon
Rāma: the hero; eldest son of King of Ayodhya
Rāvana: chief of the *rākṣasas*; demon king
Sītā: the heroine; wife of Rāma
Sugrīva: king of the monkeys
Vali: brother of Sugrīva
Viradha: a demon; abductor of Sītā

The lengthy and ancient poem is a series of adventures and ordeals centred around two characters—Rāma and his wife Sītā. The story begins with the gods approaching Viṣnu in a cosmic sleep with the request that he return to earth in human form to help them rid the world of the demon king Rāvana. So Viṣnu descends to earth as Rāma, the eldest of four sons of the King of Ayodhya (in India), destined to succeed his father. However, the second wife of the King of Ayodhya asks for Rāma to be sent into exile so that her own son could be the successor to the throne. The king complies with her wish and sends Rāma and his beautiful wife Sītā (who is the counterpart for Viṣnu's consort, the goddess Lakṣmī) into the forest, accompanied by Rāma's brother Lakṣmana. When the king eventually dies, Rāma does not return to his kingdom but remains with Sītā and Lakṣmana in the forest where they live as ascetics and encounter many strange adventures. One such episode is depicted in the West Gallery of Angkor Wat where a *rākṣasa* called Viradha seizes Sītā and, just as he is about to devour her, Rāma and Lakṣmana appear in time to save Sītā and slay the monster.

Rāvana, the demon king (whom Viṣnu had taken earthly form to destroy) is the ruler of the *rākṣasas* in the neighbouring kingdom of Lankā (Sri Lanka). His terrifying form is distinguished by 10 heads and 20 arms. Captivated by the beauty of Sītā one day he uses his power to have her kidnapped. He enlists Marica, the *rākṣasa*, to help him separate Sītā from the two brothers. Marica appears before them in the form of a golden stag. When Sītā sees the beautiful illusion she urges Rāma to capture it for her. Rāma follows the stag and manages to shoot it with an arrow. As Marica is dying he takes his true form and imitates the voice of Rāma calling his brother for help. Sītā urges Lakṣmana to answer the call. Rāvana, waiting for the moment when both brothers have left and Sītā is alone, seizes her and carries her off to his palace on the island of Laṅkā. This episode is depicted in the West Gallery at Angkor Wat. Rāma and his brother try to win Sītā back through a series of battles and adventures. Hanumān, the white monkey, and his army of monkeys help them. He allies them to Sugrīva, the great monkey king, who is battling with his brother Vali. Rāma intervenes in support of Sugrīva and shoots Vali with an arrow. In return Sugrīva and his army join Rāma and Lakṣmaṇa and together they prepare to invade Laṅkā to retrieve Sītā. With a mighty bound Hanumān reaches the island of Laṅkā, gives Rāma's ring to Sītā and assures her that she will soon be free. He then sets fire to the city and returns to aid Rāma in his efforts to retrieve Sītā by force. To enable him to do this the monkey army builds a colossal bridge to the island, the remains of which purportedly are still visible.

The battle which ensues against the demons is a long one. Indrajit, 'the invisible warrior', son of Rāvaṇa, joins the battle. He wields powerful magical arrows that turn into snakes and wind around their victims like ropes. He also can assume whatever terrifying form he wishes. In the bloody battle which follows, Indrajit kills Rāma and Lakṣmaṇa. Hanumān travels to the Himalayas with lightning speed and brings back potent herbs from Medicine Hill, the scent of which is enough to restore the devastated army and the brothers back to life. Indrajit challenges the rejuvenated Lakṣmaṇa to a duel and Lakṣmaṇa manages to kill Indrajit.

Eventually Rāma and Rāvaṇa battle each other and Rāma kills his enemy with an arrow. Good is finally victorious over evil and Rāma becomes aware of his divine antecedents. He returns to the kingdom of Ayodhya and takes his rightful place on the throne. He is reunited with Sītā but suspects his wife of infidelity after she has spent 14 years with Rāvaṇa, and he rejects her. She threatens to throw herself on a burning pyre to prove enduring faithfulness to Rāma but Agni, the god of fire, spares her from the act, thus verifying her purity and Rāma and Sītā are reunited. Rāma rejects her again as rumours abound among his people of her unfaithfulness to him. He banishes her to the forest where she bears him two sons.

After many years Rāma at last recognizes his sons at an annual forest festival. He orders Sītā to be brought to him. When they meet, Sītā finally proves her innocence by calling the earth to swallow and thus hide her if her faithfulness is genuine. The earth accepts her and Rāma and Sītā are separated forever. In the Cambodian version, however, a burning pyre is prepared for Sītā and she stands amidst the flames, proving her innocence. Agni takes her from the fire and reunites the couple once and for all. This version of the myth concludes with the start of Rāma's reign in the Kingdom of Ayodhya.

BATTLE OF KURUKSHETRA
(*Location*: Angkor Wat, Gallery of Bas-Reliefs, West Gallery, *Plan* page 97) This war is

Detail of a bas-relief at Angkor Wat showing a military procession

the main subject of the Hindu epic, the *Mahābhārata*. It involves the five Pāṇḍava princes in a fight against their cousins the Kauravas. Kṛṣṇa revenges himself on his uncle by killing Kamsa and declaring himself king. He soon decides to join Balarāma and the Pāṇḍavas in a series of battles against the Kauravas. Before the final battle, Kṛṣṇa reveals his devotion to Arjuna, one of the Pāṇḍavas, and tells him that all deeds should be done with perfect detachment. A ferocious battle ensues and Balarāma dies. Kṛṣṇa retires to the forest and is killed by a hunter who mistakes him for an antelope and shoots an arrow into his heel.

CHURNING OF THE OCEAN OF MILK

(*Location*: The best known depiction of this legend is in the Gallery of Bas-Reliefs at Angkor Wat, East Gallery, *Plan* page 97) This Hindu myth centres on gods and demons who have been churning the Ocean of Milk for 1,000 years in an effort to produce an elixir that will render them immortal and incorruptible. Unsuccessful and exhausted from fighting the demons, the gods ask Viṣṇu for help. He tells them to continue the churning and to work together with, not against, the demons in helping to extract the *amṛta* (elixir of immortality).

They begin the churning again but Mount Mandara, which forms the pivot, begins to sink. Viṣṇu comes to the rescue in his reincarnation as a tortoise and offers the back of his shell as support for the mountain. The serpent Vāsuki serves as the rope and curls himself around the pivot. The body of the serpent is stretched horizontally along the gallery and held by a row of gods on one side and a row of demons on the other. They pull first in one direction and then in the other to generate the elixir. The Ocean of Milk is churned in this manner for another 1,000 years before their efforts are rewarded. The churning yields not only the elixir of immortality but many treasures including the elephant Airāvata, the *apsarās* (celestial dancers) and the goddess Lakṣmī.

At Angkor Wat, the mountain appears as a column resting on the back of Viṣṇu in the form of a magnificent tortoise with flowers carved on its shell. The top of the column spreads into a lotus. The *apsarās* born of the churning dance above the row of gods and demons. Below, fish and mythical aquatic creatures swim in the Ocean but at the centre powerful air currents tear them to shreds.

KĀMA SHOOTS AN ARROW AT ŚIVA

(*Locations*: Angkor Wat, Banteay Samre, Banteay Srei, Bayon) Śiva retires to the Himalayas to meditate and lead the life of an ascetic. His wife Pārvatī tries to attract his attention but fails and is disappointed that he does not notice her. The gods ask Kāma, God of Love, to assist Pārvatī and help her distract Śiva from his meditation. Kāma shoots one of his flowery arrows into Śiva's heart. The latter is angry and shoots a fiery ray from his frontal eye, reducing Kāma to ashes. Śiva casts his eyes on Pārvatī and is enamoured of her beauty. He marries her and she gives birth to a son named Skanda, God of War. Śiva brings Kāma, God of Love, back to life in another manifestation as the son of Kṛṣṇa.

KṚṢṆA LIFTS MOUNT GOVARDHANA
(*Locations*: Krol Kō, Prah Khan) Indra has long been worshipped by the pastoral people of India until Kṛṣṇa persuades them to stop. This enrages Indra and he sends a deluge of rain and thunder to the shepherds. Kṛṣṇa comes forth to help them and 'lifting up Mount Govardhana from its base in one hand, he holds it in the air as easily as a small child holds a mushroom'. He supports the mountain for seven days and shelters the shepherds and their flocks.

RĀVAṆA SHAKES MOUNT KAILĀSA
(*Locations*: Angkor Wat, Banteay Srei, Bayon) Rāvaṇa, king of the demons of Laṅkā (Sri Lanka) and the enemy of Rāma, goes to Mount Kailāsa, home of Śiva and his wife Pārvatī, where he tries to enter but is forbidden access. He is furious and shouts at the monkey-headed guardian, who yells back saying that Rāvaṇa's power will be destroyed by the monkeys. Rāvaṇa is so angry he raises the base of the mountain and shakes it to attract Śiva's attention. Pārvatī is frightened and hovers near her husband, seeking protection. Śiva pushes the mountain with his toe causing it to fall on Rāvaṇa and crush him under its mass. Rāvaṇa acknowledges Śiva's power and sings his praises for 1,000 years. As a reward Śiva sets him free and gives him a sword.

ŚIVA DANCES
(*Locations*: Banteay Srei, east entry tower) Śiva in his manifestation as God of Rhythm symbolizes the eternal movement of the universe and dances to regulate the destiny of the world. He sometimes tramples a demon during his rhythmic dancing.

ŚIVA GRANTS A FAVOUR TO ARJUNA
(*Locations*: Angkor Wat, Baphuon, Bayon) This legend centres on the giving of a miraculous weapon to Arjuna, an ally of Kṛṣṇa, by Śiva. Arjuna goes to the Himalayas to propitiate the gods before the outbreak of the great war of the *Mahābhārata* and practises asceticism to earn the right to possess the weapon. The hermits of the mountain are alarmed by Arjuna's excessive meditation. Śiva intervenes and assumes the disguise of a hunter. As he approaches Śiva, a demon, disguised as a boar, charges Arjuna. Both Śiva and Arjuna shoot an arrow into the boar. The two archers are angry that they both shot the boar and begin fighting but Arjuna, a mere human, has no strength against the god Śiva and faints. When he regains consciousness he recog-

nizes Śiva and prostrates before him. Śiva pardons Arjuna and gives him the magical weapon.

VIṢṆU'S COSMIC DREAM
(*Location*: Banteay Samre, Prah Khan) In this cosmic myth Viṣṇu reclines on his side on the serpent Ananta and floats on the Ocean. His upper torso rests on his elbow. His wife Lakṣmī often sits near his feet. A golden lotus emerges from the navel of Viṣṇu signifying the beginning of a new cosmic period. The lotus opens and Brahmā appears to preside over the new creation. The Reclining Viṣṇu was one of the most popular myths in Khmer art. Its elongated form is well suited to the rectangular shape of a lintel and the base of a triangular pediment.

■ BUDDHIST MYTHOLOGY
In Khmer art the Buddha is always represented in an attitude of meditation. The most common form is a seated Buddha on the coiled body of a serpent. His hands rest in his lap and the multiple heads of the serpent spread to form a hood above him; or a standing Buddha in one of several gestures of instruction indicated by the position of his hands; or a reclining Buddha lying on his right side with one hand folded under his head, the other lying along his side—a posture depicting his entry into *nirvāṇa*. Following the Mahāyāna Buddhist tradition the Buddha is sometimes dressed in princely garments with jewels and a diadem. Other characteristics are hair curls, a cranial protuberance and elongated ear lobes.

The footprints of Buddha are also seen at some temples at Angkor. They are flat stones shaped like the sole of a foot with 11 parallel lines crossed by other lines forming compartments that contain representations of a great variety of signs, the whole grouped around a central wheel.

A bodhisattva is the religious ideal of Mahāyāna Buddhism and was widely portrayed in Khmer art, especially during the late Angkor Period when that form of Buddhism was at its height of popularity. A bodhisattva is one who has achieved Enlightenment but renounces attainment of Enlightenment to return to earth and help the sufferings of all humanity. The bodhisattva typically represented in Khmer art is the Avalokiteśvara, 'the lord who looks down in compassion', known in Cambodia as Lokeśvara, 'Lord of the World'. He is signified by a small figure on the head of an image. He carries a flask, book, lotus and rosary in his four arms. Sometimes the Lokeśvara has eight arms and holds additional objects. The faces depicted on the towers of the Bayon temple are believed to represent the bodhisattva Avalokiteśvara.

LIFE OF THE BUDDHA ŚĀKYAMUNI
Buddhist representations in the Angkor Period contain a variety of scenes from the

life of the Buddha. The Buddha was born about 563 BC and given the name Siddhārtha. His surname was Gautama and because he was born into the princely clan of the Śākyas he is often called Śākyamuni. When he was born astrologers predicted that he would be either a great king or a religious leader. Throughout his childhood his father sheltered him from exposure to the outside world. At the age of 16 he married a beautiful princess and they had two sons. His first exposure to human misery and suffering occurred when he was 29 years old and was riding outside the palace grounds and encountered a sick man, a beggar, a corpse and a Hindu priest. He was so horrified that he decided to give up his royal life so that he could help save others.

He left the palace one night with his faithful groom, an event known as 'The Great Departure'. Four guard-

Bas-reliefs at the Baphuon depicting episodes of hunting and combat from Indian epics

ians of the world also accompanied him and held the hoofs of the prince's horse with their hands so that the noise of their galloping would not awaken the guards. After leaving the palace of his father the prince rode until he came to a resting place in the forest. Surrounded by his attendants the prince removed his royal attire and handed it to his groom. Then he cut off his long hair with one stroke of his sword, symbolizing his renunciation of a worldly life.

Gautama stayed in north India studying Hindu teachings and practising the life of an ascetic for six years. He then abandoned his austere life and began a period of meditation on the banks of a river in north India. Enlightenment was his ultimate achievement and bas-reliefs at Angkor record this event with skill and accuracy.

One of the events leading to the Enlightenment was his victory over the powerful demon Māra, Lord of Worldly Desire and Delusion, who tried to prevent Gautama from achieving Enlightenment by frightening him with his army of demons. He disputed Gautama's right to reign over the world and attempted to persuade him that he must give up his diamond throne. In answer, Gautama recalled his merit acquired in previous lives. Each time he had made merit he had poured water over the hands of the recipients. His accumulated merit was so great that the earth was full of the waters of his virtues. Māra required proof of this and so the goddess of earth, to certify Gautama's claims, wrung the water from her long hair and it gushed with such force that it drowned the demon army.

Gautama continued his meditation and subsequently reached his Enlightenment or *nirvāṇa*. He became known as the Buddha or Enlightened One. On the day of his Enlightenment a torrential rainfall began. He was in such deep meditation that he was unaware of the storm. The serpent Mucilinda came to shelter him. He coiled his body and formed a seat to lift the Buddha off the ground. Then he unfurled his multiple heads to protect the Buddha from the rain. Hence this popular depiction of the Buddha in Khmer art. For the rest of his life until he died at the age of 80, the Buddha travelled throughout the country helping humanity attain release from the endless cycle of rebirth.

Khmer Architecture and Art of the Angkor Period

Khmer monuments of the Angkor Period share similarities in materials, methods of construction, plans, architectural and decorative elements and symbolism. Besides monuments, bronze and stone sculptures were also part of the rich art of the Khmer. Evidence of influence from other cultures can be discerned. For example, the initial impetus was undoubtedly from India as similarities occur in architecture, decorative motifs and sculpture. Trends from the art of Java also appear, particularly on structures in the early part of the Angkor Period. There are similarities in *kālas* and *makaras* depicted on lintels and in the profiles of some of the towers. Chinese influence can be found in monuments built by Jayavarman VII in the late twelfth and early thirteenth centuries. Such features as patterns on clothes worn by the figures depicted on the reliefs, tapestry-like background patterns and market scenes at the Bayon show Chinese characteristics. Despite these waves of foreign influence, a remarkable and distinctive feature is the individuality of Khmer art. The dominance of religious principles in form and decoration resulted in earthly representations of celestial dwellings for the gods, which are unlike any other in the world.

MATERIALS

Prototypes of **wood** served as models for the early monuments of the Angkor Period. This influence is visible on lintels and the pediments of Banteay Srei and in roof forms and shapes with curved contours. An idea of the form and layout of some wooden structures can be seen on the reliefs at the Bayon (see plans pages 144 and 148).

Three main types of building material were used in Khmer architecture of the Angkor Period. The earliest monuments were built of **brick**. Each layer was secured with a vegetable-based matter rather than mortar; the latter was not used in Khmer architecture. Sometimes the bricks were carved after being put in place. The interiors of two towers at Prasat Kravan are particularly fine examples of this method. At other times the brick was covered with plaster or stucco to provide a base for delicate and detailed decoration.

Laterite, because of its abundance in the soil of Cambodia and its durability, was used for foundations, walls, roads and occasionally for entire structures. Laterite is a red rock that is soft when it is underground because of a high water content but when it is exposed to the sunlight it hardens. To prepare laterite for use, surrounding soil is removed and the laterite is smoothed and cut into blocks before being left in

Architectural Elements of a Khmer Temple

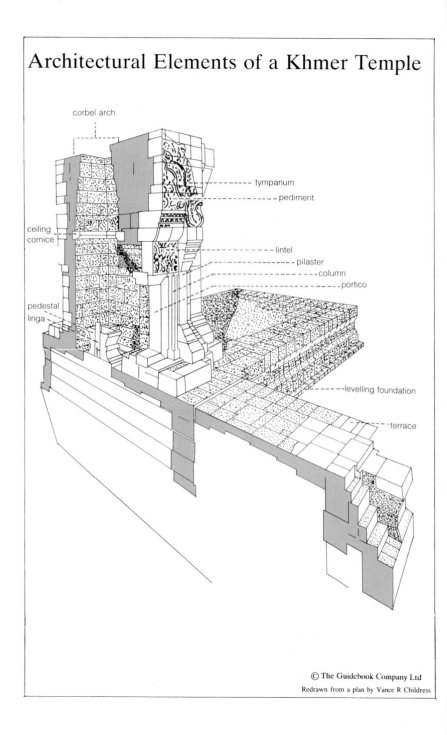

corbel arch

tympanum

pediment

ceiling cornice

lintel

pilaster

column

portico

pedestal

linga

levelling foundation

terrace

© The Guidebook Company Ltd

Redrawn from a plan by Vance R Childress

the sunlight to harden. The disadvantage of laterite is that it cannot be finely carved. **Sandstone** began to replace brick as the main building material in the late tenth century. On monuments of the early Angkor Period door frames were often cut from a single large block of stone. Evidence of this method can be seen at the upper corner on each side of the door which would otherwise reveal a join. Besides its suitability for carving, sandstone was used for roofing and the pilasters and lintels of doorways. By the eleventh century sandstone was commonly used for constructing entire temples. Sandstone quarries were located at Phnom Kulen, 40 kilometres (25 miles) northeast of Angkor. When the Tonle Sap River reversed direction the sandstone was transported on rafts along the river. The different qualities of sandstone available are reflected in the methods of construction and decorative techniques.

Both unglazed and glazed **tiles** were used for the roofs of temples. The earliest shape is a curved rectangular green-glazed tile with a protrusion on the underside that interlocked the tiles to form an overlapping pattern. The shape is similar to tiles on roofs of Chinese buildings of the tenth century.

Stucco was sometimes applied over brick and used as a medium for decoration in the early Angkor period. The composition was a mixture of lime, sand, tamarind, sugar palm and clay from a termite mound.

ARCHITECTURAL ELEMENTS

A **corbel arch** is the most primitive method of construction for spanning an opening and was the only one used by the Khmers. The corbel arch is found in both brick and sandstone structures. To build such an arch rectangular blocks are progressively cantilevered from each side until they come together. This method limits the width an arch can span and its use accounts for the narrowness found in parts of Khmer architecture such as galleries. A **false door** is a replica of an actual door and is found on a Central Sanctuary. A common example is a tower with one real door and three false doors. The intricate carving arranged in vertical panels on the doors is one of the most beautiful elements of the temple. A **lintel** is a rectangular block of sandstone placed horizontally upon a pair of pillars and over doorways. It is a principal area for decoration in Khmer temples. A **pediment** is the triangular upper portion of a wall above the portico. It is often intricately decorated with pictorial scenes. A **pillar** is a free-standing upright section that gives support in corridors and porches. In contrast, a **pilaster** is a column used on the side of an open doorway that projects slightly from the wall. A **tympanum** is the triangular space above the lintel of the doorway and is enclosed by the mouldings of the pediment. A **window with balusters**, usually between five and seven, and turned like wood or bamboo, is a hallmark of Khmer art. In the Bayon period the upper half of the window was closed with blocks of laterite and there were balusters on the lower half. This arrangement gives the appearance of a window with a lowered blind.

Line drawing of a false door with decorative centre panel and a pattern of rosettes

EVOLUTION OF THE ARCHITECTURAL PLAN

The fundamental element of Khmer architecture is a central **tower**. It was almost always oriented to the east. The simplest form is square, made of brick, with a door opening to the east, and with false doors on the other three sides. The profile of the tower is cone-shaped, created by a series of tiers gradually tapering to a softly rounded point at the top. On the earlier temples of the Angkor Period the tiers were miniature replicas of the façade of the sanctuary, whereas the tiers on temples built at a later date display other decorative features. The exterior of the tower was usually decorated but the interior was plain, perhaps to focus on the sacred image of the temple which was housed inside the sanctuary. The tower was often elevated on a square base with tiers and enclosed by a wall intercepted in the middle of each side with an **entry tower** (*gopura*). An example of a single sanctuary temple is Baksei Chamkrong (page 118).

The plan of the tower became increasingly complex in proportion to the expanded size in the Angkor Period and new requirements gradually changed the arrangement of space and volume.

A natural development of the single tower was to build between three and six brick towers, all similar in size and form, and align them in one or two rows on ground level or on a low terrace. A curious characteristic of this form is that the towers are usually unevenly spaced. The central tower is generally slightly taller than the others. Figures modelled in stucco on top of the brick were typical. This type of temple arrangement is often dedicated to ancestors of the king. Lolei and Prah Kō (page 186) of the Roluos group are examples of this type of layout.

In the next stage of development, five towers were arranged like the dots on a die on the top level of a platform with tiers. This formation is sometimes called a quincunx and symbolizes the five peaks of Mount Meru. The platform was accentuated by a stairway on each side. Access to these larger complexes was often made more dramatic by long causeways, steps and terraces highlighted with carved guardian figures such as lions and elephants. Some typical five-towered temples are Bakheng, Pre Rup and East Mebon.

Both the enclosure and the entry tower expanded in size and complexity as the architectural form developed. Concurrently, the importance of the Central Sanctuary decreased as the horizontal dimension of the temple expanded. Long halls with wooden roofs were added around the temple. Later these became continuous galleries. Other buildings such as halls for meditation and libraries complemented the area around a temple. Pavilions in the corners of each tier increased the complexity of the temple. Elaborate porches, sandstone galleries with pillars, and tiled roofs were common in the late Angkor Period. As the form developed the buildings and enclosures

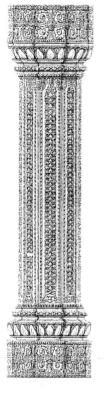

Elaborately decorated pillar with a band of lotus petals at the top and bottom

were connected with galleries. The walls of the structures were decorated profusely with motifs carved in relief. This form culminates in the art and architecture of the temple of Angkor Wat.

A synthesis of the previous styles appeared in the late twelfth century and characterizes the Buddhist temples built at that time. It was a complex architectural layout constructed at ground level with a central tower and auxiliary structures including interconnected galleries and rooms. Examples are Banteay Kdei, Prah Khan and Ta Prohm (plans page 120, 171 and 194 respectively).

Entrance towers with a gigantic face carved on four sides were a unique Khmer design of the late twelfth and early thirteenth centuries. The gates of the city of Angkor Thom are an example of this form. (For a detailed description of the towers with faces see pages 135 and 141).

The so-called **library** is a Khmer innovation. These rectangular buildings usually appear in pairs opposite each other and are placed outside the sacred enclosure, often in the courtyard. Their function is unknown but they may have served as a store room for offerings and sacred objects. The designation 'library' originated with French archaeologists who discovered scenes from a Hindu legend of the 'Nine Planets of the Earth' carved on the stones of the libraries. Because of the association with astronomy they interpreted this to mean the building served a function associated with intellect and named it a library.

The development of Khmer architecture, as described above, is divided into stylistic periods, each one named after a principal site or a specific temple. The styles established by the French, described in this book together with their dates, kings and monuments, are:

KULEN

Date: ninth century (*c* 825–75)
King: Jayavarman II (reigned 802–50)
Monuments: the Kulen temples

PRAH KŌ

Date: last quarter of the ninth century (*c* 875–93)
King: Indravarman I (reigned 877–89)
Monuments: Prah Kō (879), Bakong (881)
Transitional: Lolei (893)

BAKHENG

Date: late ninth century–early tenth century (*c* 893–925)
King: Yaśovarman I (reigned 889–900)

Line drawing of decoration on a pilaster with a female divinity

Monuments: Bakheng (893), Phnom Krom
Transitional: Baksei Chamkrong, Prasat Kravan (921)

KOH KER
Date: middle of the tenth century (*c* 921–45)
King: Jayavarman IV (reigned *c* 921–42)
Monuments: the Koh Ker Group

PRE RUP
Date: middle of the tenth century (*c* 947–65)
King: Rājendravarman II (reigned 944–68)
Monuments: East Mebon (952), Pre Rup (961)

BANTEAY SREI
Date: last half of the tenth century (*c* 967–1000)
King: Rājendravarman II and Jayavarman V
Monuments: Banteay Srei (967)

KLEANG
Date: late tenth century–early eleventh century (*c* 965–1010)
King: Jayavarman V (reigned 968–1001)
Monuments: Ta Keo (*c* 1000), North and South Kleangs, Phimeanakas (*c* 970)

BAPHUON
Date: middle of the eleventh century (*c* 1010–80)
King: Sūryavarman I (reigned 1002–50), Udayadityavarman II (reigned 1050–66)
Monuments: Baphuon, West Mebon

ANGKOR WAT
Date: twelfth century (*c* 1100–75)
King: Sūryavarman II (reigned 1113–*c* 50)
Monuments: Prah Palilay, Chau Say Tevoda, Thommanon, Banteay Samre,
Angkor Wat (1113–50)

BAYON
Date: last quarter of the twelfth and early thirteenth century (*c* 1177–1230)
King: Jayavarman VII (reigned 1181–*c* 1220)
Monuments: Banteay Kdei (1181), Ta Prohm (1186), Prah Khan (1191), Ta Som,
Angkor Thom Enclosure and Gates, Bayon (*c* 1200), Royal Terraces,
Srah Srang, Neak Pean

Bas-Reliefs
For a detailed description of the bas-reliefs see Angkor Wat, pages 96–108, and the Bayon, pages 142–150.

Cosmology in Khmer Architecture
The layout, architecture and decoration of Khmer temples were modelled according to a series of magical and religious beliefs. Khmer art echoes the cosmological themes of Hindu mythology. Certain elements are basic instruments of all rites and ceremonies whether Hindu or Buddhist. States were patterned on the order of the cosmos and linked to sacred and secular orders. One moved from the mundane world toward a spiritual one by approaching its axis from one of the four quarters. A ruler and a capital were at the centre of the universe. Cosmological and magical symbols expressed royal power. Angkor is in harmony with natural cosmic order.

The temple as a microcosm of a central mountain was an essential concept that had a profound influence on Khmer art. It occurs in both Hindu and Buddhist mythology and although the conditions vary slightly, the general ideas are the same. According to legend, the world consisted of a central continent. In the exact centre of this continent there was a cosmic mountain, known as Mount Meru, which marked the axis of the world and held up the heavens. It is associated with the Himalayas in Central Asia. Six or seven concentric chains of mountains surround Meru and represent successive stages towards knowledge; these are separated by the same number of oceans. A large stone wall encloses the outer 'Ocean of Infinity' and symbolizes the mountains around the earth. The surrounding moat represents the Oceans. In the Buddhist system, there is a continent in the form of an island beyond the ocean in each of the four cardinal regions of space. There are layers of heavens above the mountain. Gods or rulers live at the summit of Mount Meru. Fantastic animals live in the forest at the base of the mountain. It also serves as a refuge for ascetics to meditate. In Buddhism, it is the residence of the four rulers of the cardinal points. In Hinduism, Meru is ruled by Indra and is the mythical dwelling of Brahmā and other gods. The mountain is surrounded by eight guardians at each of the cardinal points.

In the early Angkor Period the temple-mountain built by each king manifested the symbolical significance of the three essentials of cosmology into architecture—the microcosm of the magical Mount Meru; enclosed by a stone wall and surrounded by a moat representing the cosmic ocean. The causeway leading up to many of the temples symbolizes a bridge between man and the gods.

Early sites were built on natural mountains but later when capitals were situated in the plains artificial mounds were constructed. They were given additional height by the architectural feature of a tiered platform. This was a Khmer innovation, unknown in India. When a *liṅga* was placed on top of the mountain its symbolism

(following pages) *Scenes of Judgement by Yama and torturers delivering punishments in hell, South Gallery of Bas-reliefs at Angkor Wat*

changed to become a representation of Mount Kailāsa, the dwelling of Śiva, even though all the other cosmological features remained.

The four directions are assigned astrological values. East, the direction of the rising sun, is auspicious and represents life. Sexually it symbolizes the creative prowess of the male. Most Khmer temples were built with the entrance facing east. In opposition, west is inauspicious, representing death, impurity, the setting sun, and sexually the female. The north is auspicious and associated with the elephant because of its strength. South is a neutral value.

Numbers are considered an expression of the structure of the universe and a means of effecting the interplay between the gods and man. Although numerous mathematical schemes have been put forth to explain the proportional measurements of specific temples, their authenticity is uncertain. It is likely the Khmers adhered to the Hindu belief that a temple must be built correctly according to a mathematical system in order for it to function in harmony with the universe. Thus if the measurements of the temple are perfect then there will also be perfection in the universe.

Under the surface of the earth are numerous hells and above it are paradises or heavens. The hells do not correspond to the one in Christianity. Hell in Khmer cosmology is a place of suffering where the damned expiate their sins and crimes and each hell is more horrific than the last. Afterwards they are reborn to begin a new life. In the Gallery of Bas-reliefs at Angkor Wat (south wall) the sins and the punishments of its 32 hells are depicted. There are also numerous paradises above the earth and above the last one is *nirvāṇa*. The duration of life in these paradises increases with the height of each one. Earth is a neutral place.

SCULPTURE

The concept of an image sculpted in the round was a part of Khmer art throughout history. The identification of a king with a deity was the core of religious belief. Remarkable sculptures in stone produced during the Angkor Period reflect the profound dedication of the art to religious causes. Bronze figures and artefacts, particularly of the twelfth century, reinforce the artistic genius of the Khmers. In 1936 the torso of a gigantic bronze statue 119 centimetres (46 inches) in height, dating to the late eleventh century, was discovered in the West Baray. The estimated length of the entire figure is 6 metres (20 feet), making it the largest figure of Khmer art ever found and arguably one of the greatest pieces ever cast in bronze in Southeast Asia. The Buddha appeared to a villager in a dream and told him about this statue and its location. Following this hint excavations led to the torso. Only the head and part of the torso have been found but the four arms and posture of this image suggest it is Viṣṇu reclining on a serpent.

Stone sculpture of the Angkor Period evolved from a pre-Angkor style that showed an elegant form and refined detail at an early date. It followed closely the style of the Indian Gupta art. Identifying characteristics of early images are a profile that is slightly S-shaped rather than frontal, clothing carved in very low relief and seemingly diaphanous, and accurately rendered anatomical details.

The features of early Khmer art continued to develop in the Angkor Period. Sculptures became increasingly more Khmer and less Indian in their form and detail. Male figures show virility and fitness where female forms are more sensuous. Guidelines to characteristics of the various artistic styles of sculpture follow:

Mid-eighth century to mid-ninth century: an architectonic rigidity; the parts of the body (head, torso, legs) are distinctly defined; deep incising; either a vertical or horizontal direction. Dress: male loin cloth is draped over left thigh in pocket-like fold and in front in the shape of an anchor.

Mid-tenth century to mid-eleventh century: the profile is unified; the figures have a sense of softness; less emphasis on drapery and headdress; lightly incised edges in the lower garments.

Twelfth century: sculpture of this period was superseded by attention to bas-reliefs and images in bronze.

Late twelfth century to early thirteenth century: the spreading nāga hood, giant heads of demons and gods, and colossal faces on towers were prominent motifs.

PART II

THE MONUMENTS

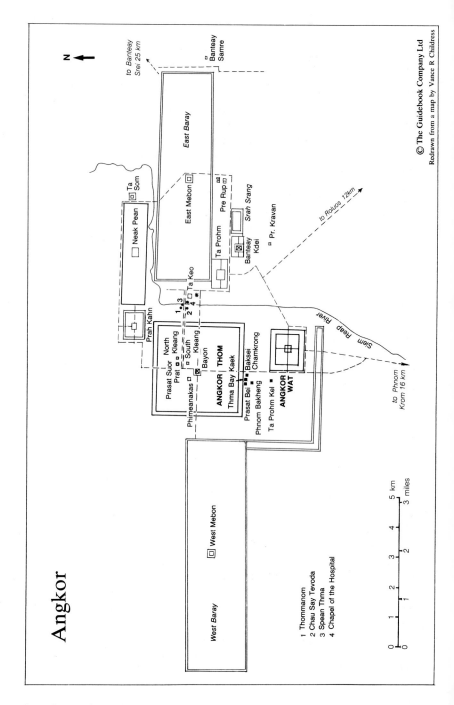

Angkor

N →

West Baray

West Mebon

East Baray

Neak Pean

Ta Som

East Mebon

Ta Prohm

Pre Rup

Srah Srang

Pr. Kravan

Banteay Kdei

Ta Keo

to Banteay Srei 25 km

Banteay Samre

Prah Kahn

1 3
2 4

Prasat Suor Prat

North Kleang

South Kleang

Phimeanakas

Bayon

ANGKOR THOM

Thma Bay Kaek

Baksei Chamkrong

Prasat Bei

Phnom Bakheng

Ta Prohm Kel

ANGKOR WAT

to Roluos 12km

Siem Reap River

to Phnom Krom 16 km

1 Thommanom
2 Chau Say Tevoda
3 Spean Thma
4 Chapel of the Hospital

0   1   2   3   4   5 km
0   1   2   3 miles

© The Guidebook Company Ltd
Redrawn from a map by Vance R Childress

(preceding page) *Detail of a celestial nymph at Ta Prohm*

Introduction

This section of the book is intended as a guide for visiting the monuments at Angkor. It can be either read in advance of a visit or afterwards to reinforce the experience, or used at the sites to enable the visitor to be an active spectator. Historical quotes from early visitors to Angkor are included where appropriate to try to capture the spirit of its past glory. Legends and symbolism are also included whenever feasible to give the visitor additional background for a better appreciation of Angkor.

VISITING THE MONUMENTS

Some suggested itineraries are given in Appendix I. They are based on the amount of time the visitor has to spend at Angkor and take into consideration the roads, proximity of the temples, and favourable light conditions. For some temples it is important to begin at the principal entrance to perceive the space and decoration as the builder intended, and entrances are indicated in the text. The monuments are oriented according to the four points of a compass which can be used as a point of reference. The temple of Angkor Wat is covered in detail in this book because of its importance, complexity and size.

Angkor provides wonderful photographic opportunities. The monuments and the surrounding jungle afford unlimited textural and lighting opportunities for composing a picture. Clouds are common and tend to diffuse the light—which is somewhat flat even though it is intense. As most of the temples face east the best lighting conditions are in the morning, except for Angkor Wat where the best light is in the afternoon because it faces west. The temples surrounded by jungle such as Ta Prohm and Prah Khan can be photographed with good results when the sun is directly overhead and shining through the foliage. Just as one is never prepared for the enormous size and overwhelming beauty of Angkor, one is never ready to leave it. With photographs and visions etched in memory, 'one need never say good-by to Angkor, for its magic will go with you wherever fate and the gods may take you to colour your thoughts and dreams to life's very end'.[1]

The names of the monuments at Angkor are often modern ones designated by Cambodians or early European travellers.

In publications by the French the enclosures of a temple are numbered starting from the central sanctuary and progressing towards the enclosing walls. The system used in this book reverses the order for the convenience of the visitor. Thus the first enclosing wall the visitor encounters when entering a temple is number one. The numbers ascend from the exterior to the interior of the monument. In many instances, though, only traces of the enclosing walls, particularly the outer one, remain.

---

[1] H W Ponder, *Cambodian Glory: The Mystery of the Deserted Khmer Cities and their Vanquished Splendour; and a Description of Life in Cambodia today* (Thornton Butterworth, London, 1936), p 316.

(following pages) *South entry tower to the royal city of Angkor Thom with a row of stone demons*

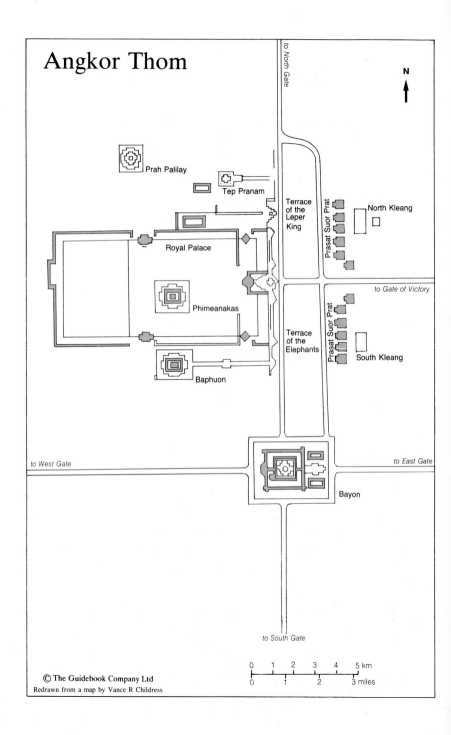

Angkor Thom

N

to North Gate

Prah Palilay

Tep Pranam

Terrace of the Leper King

Prasat Suor Prat

North Kleang

Royal Palace

to Gate of Victory

Phimeanakas

Terrace of the Elephants

Prasat Suor Prat

South Kleang

Baphuon

to West Gate

to East Gate

Bayon

to South Gate

© The Guidebook Company Ltd
Redrawn from a map by Vance R Childress

| 0 | 1 | 2 | 3 | 4 | 5 km |
| 0 | | 1 | | 2 | 3 miles |

Angkor Thom

*Angkor Thom is undeniably an expression of the highest genius. It is, in three
dimensions and on a scale worthy of an entire nation, the materialization of
Buddhist cosmology, representing ideas that only great painters would dare
to portray.*[2]

Location: 1,700 metres (1,554 yards) north of Angkor Wat
Access: Enter and leave Angkor Thom by the south, north or Victory gates
Date: End of the 12th century–beginning of the 13th century
King: Jayavarman VII
Religion: Buddhist
Art Style: Bayon

BACKGROUND

Angkor Thom, the last capital of the Khmer Empire, was a fortified city enclosing
residences of priests, officials of the palace and military, as well as buildings for administering the kingdom. These structures were built of wood and have perished but
the remaining stone monuments testify that Angkor Thom was indeed a 'Great City',
as its name implies. Temples inside the walls of the city described in this book are:
Bayon, Baphuon, Phimeanakas, Terrace of the Elephants, Terrace of the Leper King,
Prah Palilay, Tep Pranam and Prasat Suor Prat.

The Royal Palace situated within the city of Angkor Thom is of an earlier date and
belonged to kings of the tenth and first half of the eleventh centuries. Although the
foundations and an enclosing wall around the palace with entry towers have been
identified, little evidence remains of the layout of the buildings inside the enclosure.
This absence of archaeological evidence of the royal buildings suggests that they were
constructed of wood and have perished. The French ascertained a general plan of the
Royal Palace (see map opposite). It included the temple-mountain of Phimeanakas
and surrounding pools together with residences and buildings for administering the
capital which were probably at the back of the enclosure. Jayavarman VII reconstructed the original site of the Royal Palace to erect the city of Angkor Thom which was
centred on the temple of Bayon and surrounded by a wall.

Zhou Daguan, the Chinese emissary who provided the only first-hand account of
the Khmers, described the splendour of Angkor Thom:

[2]   J Boisselier, 'The Symbolism of Angkor Thom', H S H Subhadradis Diskul and V di Crocco trans, text of lecture
given at the Siam Society on 17 November 1987, in *Siam Society Newsletter*, Vol 4, No 1, p 3.

> At the center of the Kingdom rises a Golden Tower [Bayon] flanked by
> more than twenty lesser towers and several hundred stone chambers. On
> the eastern side is a golden bridge guarded by two lions of gold, one on
> each side, with eight golden Buddhas spaced along the stone chambers.
> North of the Golden Tower of Bronze [Baphuon], higher even than the
> Golden Tower: a truly astonishing spectacle, with more than ten chambers
> at its base. A quarter of a mile further north is the residence of the King.
> Rising above his private apartments is another tower of gold. These are the
> monuments which have caused merchants from overseas to speak so often
> of 'Cambodia the rich and noble'.[3]

Symbolically, Angkor Thom is a microcosm of the universe, divided into four
parts by the main axes. The temple of the Bayon is situated at the exact centre of the
axes and stands as the symbolical link between heaven and earth. The wall enclosing
the city of Angkor Thom represents the stone wall around the universe and the
mountain ranges around Meru. The surrounding moat (now dry) symbolizes the
cosmic ocean.

LAYOUT
The city of Angkor Thom consists of a square, each side of which is about three kilometres (1.9 miles) long. A laterite wall 8 metres (26 feet) in height around the city
encloses an area of 145.8 hectares (360 acres). A moat with a width of 100
metres (328 feet) surrounds the outer wall. An entry tower and a long causeway
bisect each side of the wall except on the east where there are two entrances. The
additional one, called the 'Gate of Victory', is aligned with the causeway leading to the
Terraces of the Elephants and the Leper King. A small temple known as 'Prasat
Chrung' stands at each corner of the wall around the city of Angkor Thom. An earth
embankment 25 metres (82 feet) wide supports the inner side of the wall and serves
as a road around the city.

CAUSEWAY WITH STONE FIGURES
A long causeway leading to each entry tower is flanked by a row of 54 stone figures
on each side—demons on the right and gods on the left—to make a total of 108
mythical beings guarding the city of Angkor Thom. The demons have a grimacing
expression and wear a military headdress whereas the gods look serene with their
almond-shaped eyes and wear a conical headdress. (Some of the heads on these figures are copies; the original ones have been removed and are at the Angkor Conservancy in Siem Reap.)

A serpent spreads its nine heads in the shape of a fan at the beginning of the causeway. Its body extends the length of the causeway and is held by the gods and demons forming a serpent-like railing. It may symbolize the rainbow uniting the worlds of man and the gods. This representation is reinforced by the presence of Indra.

A small sandstone temple dedicated to the bodhisattva Avalokiteśvara occupies each corner of the wall enclosing the city of Angkor Thom. An inscription at the temple names Jayavarman VII as the builder and gives the charter of the foundation of the wall and moat of the city. Each temple is in the shape of a cross, opens to the east with a porch on each side, and is crowned with a lotus-shaped top. A base with two tiers supports the temple. Female figures in niches and false windows typical of the period decorate the exterior. The upper half of the window is sealed with laterite blocks in emulation of an awning; the lower half contains balusters.

ENTRY TOWERS
'Through here all comers to the city had to pass, and in honour of this function it has been built in a style grandiose and elegant, forming a whole, incomparable in its strength and expression.'[4]

The five entry towers are among the most photographed of all the ancient Cambodian ruins. Each sandstone tower rises 23 metres (75 feet) to the sky and is crowned with four heads, one facing each cardinal direction. The faces may represent the rulers of the four cardinal points at the summit of Mount Meru.

The lower half of each gate is modelled like an elephant with three heads. Their trunks, which serve as pillars, are plucking lotus flowers. The Hindu god Indra sits at the centre of the elephant with an *apsarā* on each side. He holds a thunderbolt in his lower left hand.

Looking through the tower one can see a corbel arch, a hallmark of Khmer architecture. Inside, wooden crossbeams are visible and a sentry box stands on each side.

[3]   Chou Ta-Kuan (Zhou Daguan), *The Customs of Cambodia*, p 2.
[4]   P J de Beerski, *Angkor: Ruins in Cambodia*, p 52.

Angkor Wat: 'the city which is a temple'

Angkor Wat, in its beauty and state of preservation, is unrivaled. Its mightiness and magnificence bespeak a pomp and a luxury surpassing that of a Pharaoh or a Shah Jahan, an impressiveness greater than that of the Pyramids, an artistic distinctiveness as fine as that of the Taj Mahal.[5]

Location: Six kilometres (four miles) north of Siem Reap; south of Angkor Thom

Access: Enter and leave Angkor Wat from the west

Date: Angkor Wat was built in the first half of the 12th century (1113–5). Estimated time for construction of the temple is 30 years.

King: Sūryavarman II

Religion: Hindu (dedicated to Viṣṇu)

Art Style: Angkor Wat

The Cambodian flag takes the towers of Angkor Wat as a national symbol

BACKGROUND

Angkor Wat, the largest monument of the Angkor group and the best preserved, is an architectural masterpiece. Its perfection in composition, balance, proportions, reliefs and sculpture make it one of the finest monuments in the world.

Wat is the Thai name for 'temple' (the French spelling is 'vat'), which was probably added to 'Angkor' when it became a Theravāda Buddhist monument, most likely in the sixteenth century (for the etymology of the name 'Angkor' see page 17). After 1432 when the capital moved to Phnom Penh, Angkor Wat was cared for by Buddhist monks.

It is generally accepted that Angkor Wat was a funerary temple for King Sūryavarman II and oriented to the west to conform with the symbolism between the setting sun and death. The bas-reliefs, designed for viewing from left to right in the order of Hindu funereal ritual, support this function.

ARCHITECTURAL PLAN

The plan of Angkor Wat is difficult to grasp when walking through the monument because of the vastness. Its complexity and beauty both attract and distract one's attention. From a distance Angkor Wat appears to be a colossal mass of stone on one level with a long causeway leading to the centre but close up it is a series of elevated towers, covered galleries, chambers, porches and courtyards on different levels linked by stairways.

The height of Angkor Wat from the ground to the top of the central tower is greater than it might appear: 213 metres (699 feet), achieved with three rectangular or square levels (1–3). Each one is progressively smaller and higher than the one below, starting from the outer limits of the temple. Covered galleries with columns define the boundaries of the first and second levels.

The third level supports five towers—four in the corners and one in the middle—and these are the most prominent architectural feature of Angkor Wat. This arrangement is sometimes called a quincunx. Graduated tiers, one rising above the other, give the towers a conical shape and, near the top, rows of lotuses taper to a point. The overall profile imitates a lotus bud.

Several architectural lines stand out in the profile of the monument. The eye is drawn left and right to the horizontal aspect of the levels and upward to the soaring height of the towers. The ingenious plan of Angkor Wat only allows a view of all five towers from certain angles. They are not visible, for example, from the entrance. Many of the structures and courtyards are in the shape of a cross. The visitor should study the plan on page 86 and become familiar with this dominant layout. A curved sloping roof on galleries, chambers and aisles is a hallmark of Angkor Wat. From a distance it looks like a series of long narrow ridges but close up the form identifies itself. It is a roof made of gracefully arched stone rectangles placed end to end. Each row of tiles is capped with an end tile at right angles along the ridge of the roof. The scheme culminates in decorated tympanums with elaborate frames.

Steps provide access to the various levels. Helen Churchill Candee, who visited Angkor in the 1920s, thought their usefulness surpassed their architectural purpose. The steps to Angkor Wat 'are made to force a halt at beauteous obstructions that the mind may be prepared for the atmosphere of sanctity', she wrote.[6]

In order to become familiar with the composition of Angkor Wat the visitor should learn to recognize the repetitive elements in the architecture. Galleries with columns, towers, curved roofs, tympanums, steps and the cross-shaped plan occur again and again. It was by combining two or more of these aspects that a sense of height was achieved. This arrangement was used to link one part of the monument to another. Roofs were frequently layered to add height, length or dimension. A smaller replica of the central towers was repeated at the limits of two prominent areas—the galleries and the entry pavilions. The long causeway at the entrance reappears on the other side of the entry pavilion.

5   D H Dickason, *Wondrous Angkor*, (Kelly & Walsh, Shanghai, 1937), p 46.

6   H Churchill Candee, *Angkor: The Magnificent, The Wonder City of Ancient Cambodia*, p 71.

Ground Plan of Angkor Wat

N ←

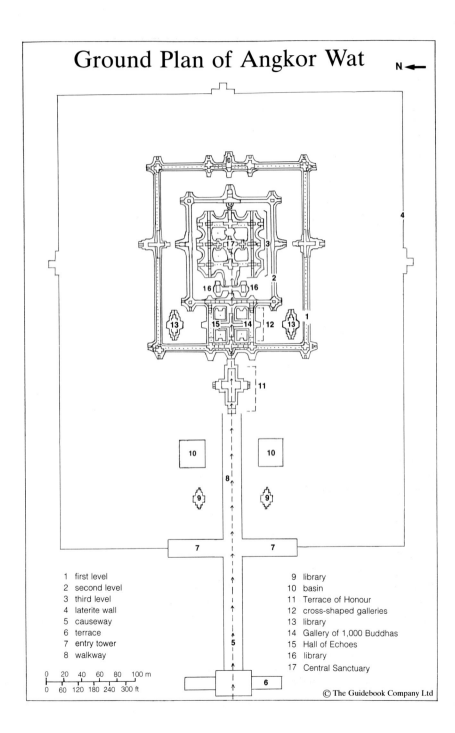

1 first level
2 second level
3 third level
4 laterite wall
5 causeway
6 terrace
7 entry tower
8 walkway

9 library
10 basin
11 Terrace of Honour
12 cross-shaped galleries
13 library
14 Gallery of 1,000 Buddhas
15 Hall of Echoes
16 library
17 Central Sanctuary

0   20   40   60   80   100 m
0   60   120   180   240   300 ft

© The Guidebook Company Ltd

SYMBOLISM

Angkor Wat is a miniature replica of the universe in stone and represents an earthly model of the cosmic world. The central tower rises from the centre of the monument symbolizing the mythical mountain, Meru, situated at the centre of the universe. Its five towers correspond to the peaks of Meru. The outer wall corresponds to the mountains at the edge of the world, and the surrounding moat the oceans beyond.

LAYOUT

Even though Angkor Wat is the most photographed Khmer monument, nothing approaches the actual experience of seeing this temple. Frank Vincent grasped this sensation over 100 years ago:

> *The general appearance of the wonder of the temple is beautiful and romantic as well as impressive and grand...it must be seen to be understood and appreciated.*[7]

Helen Churchill Candee experienced a similar reaction some 50 years later:

> *One can never look upon the ensemble of the Vat without a thrill, a pause, a feeling of being caught up into the heavens. Perhaps it is the most impressive sight in the world of edifices.*[8]

Angkor Wat occupies a rectangular area of about 208 hectares (500 acres) defined by a laterite wall (4). The first evidence of the site is a moat with a long sandstone causeway (length 250 metres, 820 feet; width 12 metres, 39 feet) crossing it and serving as the main access to the monument (5). The moat is 200 metres (656 feet) wide with a perimeter of 5.5 kilometres (3.4 miles).

The west entrance begins with steps leading to a raised sandstone terrace (6) in the shape of a cross at the foot of the long causeway. Giant stone lions on each side of the terrace guard the monument.

Looking straight ahead, one can see at the end of the causeway the entry gate with three towers of varying heights and with collapsed upper portions (7). This entry tower hides the full view of the five towers of the central group. A long covered gallery with square columns and a curved roof extends along the moat to the left and right of the entry tower. This is the majestic façade of Angkor Wat and a fine example

---

[7] F Vincent, *The Land of the White Elephant: Sights and Scenes in South-East Asia 1871–1872* (Oxford University Press, Singapore, rep, 1988), pp 209–11.

[8] H Churchill Candee, *Angkor: The Magnificent, The Wonder City of Ancient Cambodia*, pp 68–9.

of classical Khmer architecture. Helen Churchill Candee must have been standing on this terrace almost 70 years ago when she wrote:

> *Any architect would thrill at the harmony of the façade, an unbroken stretch of repeated pillars leading from the far angles of the structure to the central opening which is dominated by three imposing towers with broken summits.*[9]

This façade originally had another row of pillars with a roof. Evidence of this remains in a series of round holes set in square bases in front of the standing pillars.

Tip: Before proceeding along the causeway, turn right, go down the steps of the terrace and walk along the path a few metres for a view of all five towers of Angkor Wat. Return to the centre of the terrace and walk down the causeway towards the main part of the temple. The left-hand side of the causeway has more original sandstone than the right-hand side which was restored by the French. In the 1920s when R J Casey walked on this causeway he noted it was 'an oddity of engineering.... The slabs were cut in irregular shapes, which meant that each had to be chiselled to fit the one adjoining. The effect as seen under the noonday sun...is like that of a long strip of watered silk'.[10]

On the left side just before the midway point in the causeway two large feet are carved in a block of sandstone. They belong to one of the figures at the entrances to Angkor Thom and were brought to Angkor Wat in this century when the causeway was repaired with reused stones.

The causeway leads to the cross-shaped entry tower (7) mentioned earlier. The upper portions of the three sections on this tower—one each at the centre and the two ends—have collapsed. The porches on each end of the gallery may have served as passages for elephants, horses and carts as they are on ground level. When Helen Churchill Candee saw these entrances in the 1920s she remarked that 'architecture made to fit the passage of elephants is an idea most inspiriting'.[11] A figure of a standing Viṣṇu (eight arms) is on the right inside the entry tower. Traces of original colour can be seen on the ceiling of the entry tower at the left.

Continue westward along a second raised walkway (length 350 metres, 1,148 feet; width 9 metres, 30 feet) (8). A low balustrade resembling the body of a serpent borders each side. Short columns support the balustrade. Looking west one sees the celebrated view of Angkor Wat that appears on the Cambodian flag. Standing at this

[9] H Churchill Candee, *Angkor: The Magnificent, The Wonder City of Ancient Cambodia*, p 25.
[10] R J Casey, *Four Faces of Śiva: The Detective Story of a Vanished Race*, p 200.
[11] H Churchill Candee, *Angkor: The Magnificent, The Wonder City of Ancient Cambodia*, p 73.

The interior courtyard of the second level gallery of Angkor Wat, Garnier, 1873

point one feels compelled to 'get to the wondrous group of the five domes, companions of the sky, sisters of the clouds, and determine whether or not one lives in a world of reality or in a fantastic dream'.[12]

Six pairs of ceremonial stairs with platforms on each side of the walkway lead to the courtyard. A continuation of the serpent balustrade along the walkway frames the stairs. This arrangement is sometimes called a **landing platform**. The balustrade terminates with the body of the serpent making a turn at right angles towards the sky and gracefully spreading its nine heads to form the shape of a fan.

Two buildings, so-called **libraries** (9), stand in the courtyard on the left and right, just past the middle of the causeway. These 'jewel-boxes of Khmer art' are perfectly formed. A large central area, four porches, columns and steps present a symmetrical plan in the shape of a cross. Some of the columns have been replaced with cement copies for support. An original pillar lies on the ground before the library on the left.

In front of the libraries are two basins (length 65 metres, 213 feet; width 50 metres, 164 feet) (**10**). The one on the left is filled with water whereas the other one is usually dry. **Tip**: Turn left at the

Elevation of the western façade of Angkor Wat including the five towers and the Gallery of Bas-reliefs

first steps after the library and before the basin and follow the path for about 40 metres (131 feet) to a large tree for a superb view of the five towers of Angkor Wat, particularly at sunrise.

The walkway leads to a terrace in the shape of a cross, known as the **Terrace of Honour**, just in front of the principal entry tower of Angkor Wat (**11**). Supporting columns and horizontal carved moulding around the base accentuate the form of the terrace. Steps flanked by lions on pedestals are on three sides of the terrace. Ritual dances were performed here and it may have been where the king viewed processions and received foreign dignitaries. R Casey sensed such activity in the 1920s:

> *One cannot but feel that only a few hours ago it was palpitating with life. The torches were burning about the altars. Companies of priests were in the galleries chanting the rituals. Dancing-girls were flitting up and down the steps...That was only an hour or two ago, monsieur...it cannot have been more.*[13]

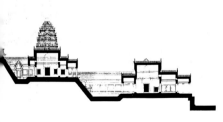

From the top of the terrace there is a fine view of the gallery on the **first level**, known as the **Gallery of Bas-reliefs** (215 by 187 metres, 705 by 614 feet) (**1**). The outer side, closest to the visitor, comprises a row of 60 columns whereas the inner side is a solid wall decorated with bas-reliefs. **Tip**: At this point the visitor has the choice of continuing straight to the central towers or turning right to see the Gallery of Bas-reliefs (see pages 96–108 for a description of the bas-reliefs).

The unit providing a link between the first and second levels is the **Cross-shaped Galleries** (**12**). This unique architectural design consists of two covered galleries with square columns in the shape of a cross and a courtyard divided into four equal parts with paved basins and steps. The method used by

[12] H Churchill Candee, *Angkor: The Magnificent, The Wonder City of Ancient Cambodia*, p 68.

[13] R J Casey, *Four Faces of Śiva: The Detective Story of a Vanished Race*, p 62.

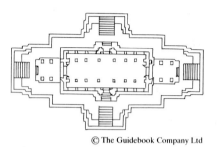

Plan of the Library

the Khmers to form corbel arches is visible in the vaults. Several decorative features in these galleries stand out: windows with balusters turned as if they were made of wood, rosettes on the vaults, a frieze of *apsarās* under the cornices, and ascetics at the base of the columns. **Tip**: Some of the pillars in the galleries of this courtyard have inscriptions written in Sanskrit and Khmer.

On either side of the courtyard there are two libraries of similar form but smaller than the ones along the entrance causeway (**13**).

The **Gallery of 1,000 Buddhas**, on the right, once contained many images dating from the period when Angkor Wat was Buddhist (**14**). Only a few of these figures remain today.

The gallery on the left is the **Hall of Echoes**, so named because of its unusual acoustics (**15**). **Tip**: To hear the resonance in the Hall of Echoes walk to the end of the gallery, stand in the left-hand corner with your back to the wall, thump your chest and listen carefully.

Those who want to visit the library (**16**) should leave by the door at the end of this gallery. There is a good view of the upper level of Angkor Wat from this library.

Return to the centre of the cross-shaped galleries and continue walking toward the central towers. Another set of stairs alerts one to the continuing ascent. The outer wall of the gallery of the **second level**, closest to the visitor, (100 by 115 metres, 328 by 377 feet), is solid and undecorated, probably to create an environment for meditation by the priests and the king (**2**).

The starkness of the exterior of the second level gallery is offset by the decoration of the interior. Over 1,500 *apsarās* ('celestial dancers') line the walls of the gallery, offering endless visual and spiritual enchantment. These graceful and beautiful females delight all visitors. They were created by the Churning of the Ocean of Milk.

When one first walks into the courtyard the multitude of female figures on the walls and in the niches may seem repetitive but as one moves closer and looks carefully one sees that every one of these celestial nymphs is different. The elaborate coiffures, headdresses and jewellery befit, yet never overpower, these 'ethereal inhabitants of the heavens'.

Apsarās appear at Angkor Wat for the first time in twos and threes. These groups break with the traditional formality of decoration in other parts of the temple by standing with arms linked in coquettish postures and always in frontal view except for the feet, which appear in profile.

Pang, a Cambodian poet, in a tribute to the Khmer ideal of female beauty wrote of the *apsarās* in the seventeenth century:

> *These millions of gracious figures, filling you with such emotion that the eye is never wearied, the soul is renewed, and the heart never sated! They were never carved by the hands of men! They were created by the Gods—living, lovely, breathing women!*[14]

Only the king and the high priest were allowed on the upper or **third level** of Angkor Wat (3). It lacks the stately covered galleries of the other two but is the base of the five central towers, one of which contains the most sacred image of the temple.

The Library at Angkor Wat is built in a symmetrical plan in the shape of a cross

---

[14]   Aymonier, trans, in *Textes Khmers*, 1878.

Dancers performing scenes from the Rāmāyana on the second causeway at the west entrance to Angkor Wat

Three of the twelve towers at Prasat Suor Prat, c. 1875

The square base (60 metres, 197 feet long) of the upper level is 13 metres (43 feet) high and rises over 40 metres (131 feet) above the second level. Twelve sets of stairs with 40 steps each—one in the centre of each side and two at the corners—ascend at a 70-degree angle giving access to this level.

Tip: The stairway to the third level is less steep on the west (centre) but those who suffer from vertigo should use the south stairway (centre), which has concrete steps and a handrail. The steps on all sides are exceptionally narrow. The visitor should ascend and descend sideways.

All the repetitive elements of the architectural composition of Angkor Wat appear on the upper level. The space is divided into a cross-shaped area defined with covered galleries and four paved courts. An entry tower with a porch and columns is at the top of each stairway. Passages supported on both sides with double rows of columns link the entry tower to the central structure. The corners of the upper level are dominated by the four towers. Steps both separate and link the different parts. A narrow covered gallery with a double row of pillars and windows and balusters on the outer side surrounds the third level.

The **Central Sanctuary** (**17**) rises on a tiered base 42 metres (137 feet) above the upper level. The highest of the five towers, it is equal in height to the cathedral of Notre Dame in Paris. This central sanctuary sheltered the sacred image of the temple. It originally had four porches opening to the cardinal directions.

The central core was walled up some time after the sacking of Angkor in the middle of the fifteenth century. Nearly 500 years later French archaeologists discovered a vertical shaft 27 metres (89 feet) below the surface in the centre of the upper level with a hoard of gold objects at the base.

At the summit the layout of Angkor Wat reveals itself at last. The view is a spectacle of beauty befitting the Khmers' architectural genius for creating harmonious proportions. **Tip**: Walk *all* the way around the outer gallery of the upper level to enjoy the view of the surrounding countryside, the causeway in the west and the central group of towers.

> *You have not quite an aerial view—the Phnom [summit] is not high enough for that...But you can see enough to realize something of the superb audacity of the architects who dared to embark upon a single plan measuring nearly a mile square. Your point of view is diagonal; across the north-west corner of the moat to the soaring lotus-tip of the central sanctuary, you can trace the perfect balance of every faultless line. Worshipful for its beauty, bewildering in its stupendous size, there is no other point from which the Wat appears so inconceivable an undertaking to have been attempted—much less achieved— by human brains and hands.*[15]

GALLERY OF BAS-RELIEFS

'By their beauty they first attract, by their strangeness they hold attention', Helen Churchill Candee wrote of the bas-reliefs in the 1920s.[16] The Gallery of Bas-reliefs, surrounding the first level of Angkor Wat, contains 1,200 square metres (12,917 square feet) of sandstone carvings. The reliefs cover most of the inner wall of all four sides of the gallery and extend for two metres (seven feet) from top to bottom. The detail, quality, composition and execution give them an unequalled status in world art. Columns along the outer wall of the gallery create an intriguing interplay of light and shadow on the reliefs. The effect is one of textured wallpaper that looks like 'the work of painters rather than sculptors'. The bas-reliefs are of 'dazzling rich decoration—always kept in check, never allowed to run unbridled over wall and ceiling; possess strength and repose, imagination and power of fantasy; wherever one looks [the] main effect is one of "supreme dignity"', wrote a visitor 50 years ago.[17]

The bas-reliefs are divided into eight sections, two on each wall of the square gallery. Each section depicts a specific theme. In addition the two pavilions at the corners of the West Gallery have a variety of scenes. This book does not include descriptions of badly damaged reliefs. Some others are unidentifiable. The composition of the reliefs can be divided into two types: scenes without any attempt to contain or separate the contents; and scenes contained in panels which are sometimes superimposed on one another—this type is probably later. The panels run horizontally along the wall and generally consist of two or three parts. Sometimes the borders at the top and bottom are also decorated.

Themes for the bas-reliefs derive from two main sources—Indian epics and sacred books and warfare of the Angkor Period. Some scholars suggest that the placement of a relief has a relevance to its theme. The reliefs on the east and west walls, for example, depict themes related to the rising and setting sun.

The word 'bas' means 'low or shallow' and refers to the degree of projection of the relief. The method of creating reliefs at Angkor Wat was generally to carve away the background leaving the design in relief. Sometimes, though, the method was reversed giving a sunken appearance.

Parts of some of the reliefs have a polished appearance on the surface. There are two theories as to why this occurred. The position of the sheen and its occurrence in important parts of the reliefs suggest it may have resulted from visitors rubbing their hands over them. Some art historians, though, think it was the result of lacquer applied over the reliefs. Traces of gilt and paint, particularly black and red, can also be

[15]   H W Ponder, *Cambodian Glory: The Mystery of the Deserted Khmer Cities and their Vanquished Splendour...* , pp 76–80.

[16]   H Churchill Candee, *Angkor: The Magnificent, The Wonder City of Ancient Cambodia*, p 92.

[17]   O Sitwell, *Escape With Me! An Oriental Sketch-Book* (Macmillan, London, 1940), p 91.

Angkor Wat: Gallery of Bas-reliefs

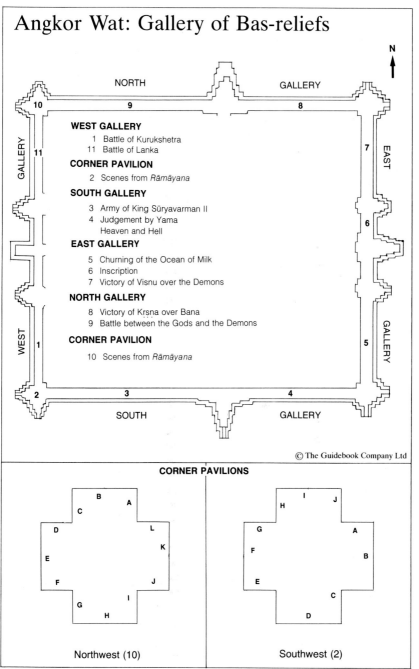

N

NORTH **GALLERY**

10   9   8

WEST GALLERY
  1 Battle of Kurukshetra
  11 Battle of Lanka
CORNER PAVILION
  2 Scenes from *Rāmāyana*
SOUTH GALLERY
  3 Army of King Sūryavarman II
  4 Judgement by Yama
     Heaven and Hell
EAST GALLERY
  5 Churning of the Ocean of Milk
  6 Inscription
  7 Victory of Visnu over the Demons
NORTH GALLERY
  8 Victory of Krsna over Bana
  9 Battle between the Gods and the Demons
CORNER PAVILION
  10 Scenes from *Rāmāyana*

WEST GALLERY   11

EAST   7   6

GALLERY   5

1

2   3   4

SOUTH **GALLERY**

CORNER PAVILIONS

B   A
C
D   L
      K
E
F   J
  G   I
    H

Northwest (10)

I   J
H
G
F   A
E   B
      C
    D

Southwest (2)

*Main part of the façade of the Terrace of the Elephants at Angkor Thom
depicting realistic hunting scenes, c. 1880*

found on some of the reliefs. They are probably the remains of an undercoat or a fixative.

Several primitive artistic conventions are seen in the **bas-reliefs**. A river is represented by two parallel vertical lines with fish swimming between them. As in Egyptian art, a person's rank is indicated by size. The higher the rank the larger the size. In battle scenes, broken shafts on the ceremonial umbrellas of a chief signify defeat. Perspective is shown by planes placed one above the other. The higher up the wall, the further away is the scene. Figures with legs far apart and knees flexed are in a flying posture.

VISITING THE GALLERY OF BAS-RELIEFS

> *Those who like to linger in this wonderful gallery of bas-reliefs will always be made happy by new discoveries and will return as often as other joys of Angkor will allow.*[18]

Tip: As the bas-reliefs at Angkor Wat were designed for viewing from right to left, the visitor should follow this convention for maximum appreciation. Enter at the west entrance, turn right into the gallery and continue walking counter-clockwise. If you start from another point always keep the monument on your left.

If one's time at Angkor is limited, the following bas-reliefs are recommended (the numbers refer to plan page 97):

Location		*Theme*
1	West Gallery	Battle of Kurukshetra
3	South Gallery	Army of King Sūryavarman II
4	South Gallery	Judgement by Yama Heaven and Hell
5	East Gallery	Churning of the Ocean of Milk
11	West Gallery	Battle of Laṅkā

Descriptions of the bas-reliefs in this guidebook follow the normal route for viewing Angkor Wat. They begin in the middle of the West Gallery and continue counter-clockwise. The other half of the West Gallery, therefore, is at the end of the section. Identifying characteristics are in parenthesis and the locations of scenes on the bas-reliefs are in bold type.

■ WEST GALLERY
BATTLE OF KURUKSHETRA
This battle scene is the main subject of the Hindu epic *Mahābhārata*. It recalls the historic wars in Kurukshetra, a province in India, and depicts the last battle between rival enemies who are cousins (see page 54 for a description of this legend).

The armies of the Kauravas and the Pandavas march from opposite ends towards the centre of the panel where they meet in combat. Headpieces differentiate the warriors of the two armies. The scene begins with infantry marching into battle and musicians playing a rhythmic cadence. The battlefield is the scene of hand-to-hand combat and many dead soldiers. Chief officers and generals (represented on a larger scale) oversee the battle in chariots and on elephants and horses. The scene builds up gradually and climaxes in a mêlée. Bisma (near the beginning of the panel), one of the heroes of the *Mahābhārata* and commander of the Kauravas, pierced with arrows, is dying and his men surround him. Arjuna (holding a shield decorated with the face of the demon Rāhu) shoots an arrow at Kṛṣṇa, his half-brother, and kills him. After death, Kṛṣṇa (four arms) becomes the charioteer of Arjuna.

---

[18]   H Churchill Candee, *Angkor: The Magnificent, The Wonder City of Ancient Cambodia*, p 101.

Commander of the Siamese army with plumed headdress and braid-like pendants

■ **CORNER PAVILION (SOUTHWEST)** Enter the pavilion and view the scenes facing you; then continue clockwise around the pavilion (see insert page 97). The bas-reliefs in this pavilion depict scenes from the life of Kṛṣṇa and from the Indian epic the *Rāmāyaṇa*.

EAST

A. **Left**: Water festival; two ships (superimposed) with *apsarās*; chess players (top ship).
Right: cockfight.

B. **Centre, above the door**: A god receiving offerings.

SOUTH

C. **Left, top to bottom**: A fight between Vali and Sugrīva, the monkey king; Rāma shoots Vali with an arrow who lies in the arms of his wife (three-pointed headdress); monkeys mourn his death (see pages 52–4 for a detailed description of this legend).

D. **Centre, above the door**: Murder of a demon; Kṛṣṇa extinguishes a fire.

WEST

E. **Left**: Śiva sits with his wife Pārvatī on Mount Kailāsa.

F. **Centre, above the door**: Kṛṣṇa uproots trees with a stone he is tied to.

G. **Right**: Rāvaṇa, disguised as a chameleon, presents himself at the palace of Indra.

NORTH

H. **Left**: The Churning of the Ocean of Milk.
Above: The sun and the moon

I. **Centre, above the door**: Rāma kills Marica, who, disguised as a golden stag, helped in the abduction of Sītā (see pages 52–4 for a description of this legend).

J. **Right**: Kṛṣṇa lifts Mount Govardhana to shelter the shepherds and their herds from the storm ignited by the anger of Indra (see page 57 for a detailed description of this legend)

■ SOUTH (HISTORICAL) GALLERY
ARMY OF KING SŪRYAVARMAN II

This gallery depicts a 'splendid triumphal procession' from a battle between the Khmers and their enemies. The reliefs show methods used in warfare, mainly hand-to-hand combat, as they had no machinery and no knowledge of firearms. The naturalistic depiction of trees and animals in the background of this panel is unusual. The central figure of this gallery is King Sūryavarman II, the builder of Angkor Wat, who appears twice. An inscription on the panel identifies him by his posthumous name, suggesting it may have been

Servant with Siamese army, after Delaporte

done after his death. The rectangular holes randomly cut in this gallery may have contained precious objects of the temple.

On the upper tier the king (seated with traces of gilt on his body) holds an audience on a mountain. Below, women of the palace walk down a mountain in the forest. The army gathers for inspection and the commanders mounted on elephants join their troops who are marching towards the enemy. The commander's rank is identified by a small inscription near the figure. King Sūryavarman II stands on an elephant (conical headdress, sword with the blade across his shoulder) and servants around him hold 15 ceremonial umbrellas. Visṇu stands on a Garuḍa on a flag pole in front of the king's elephant.

The lively and loud procession of the Sacred Fire (carried in an ark) follows with standard bearers, musicians and jesters. Brahmans chant to the accompaniment of cymbals. The royal sacrificer rides in a palanquin.

Towards the end of the panel: The military procession resumes with a troop of Thai soldiers (pleated skirts with floral pattern; belts with long pendants; plaited hair; headdresses with plumes; short moustaches) led by their commander who is mounted on an elephant. The Thai troops were probably either mercenaries or a contingent from the province of Louvo (today called Lopburi) conscripted to the Khmer army. A number of the Khmer warriors wear helmets with horns or animal heads (deer, horse, bird) and some of their shields are embellished with monsters for the same purpose.

A scene from the Rāmāyana *depicting the Battle of Laṅkā with monkey warriors fighting against the giant demons, West Gallery of Bas-reliefs at Angkor Wat*

JUDGEMENT BY YAMA; HEAVEN AND HELL

Three tiers recount the judgement of mankind by Yama and two tiers depict Heaven and Hell. Inscriptions have identified 37 heavens where one sees leisurely pursuits in palaces and 32 hells with scenes of punishment and suffering. Draperies and *apsarās* separate the two and a row of Garuḍas borders the tier on the bottom. The roof was destroyed by lightning in 1947 and subsequently the ceiling of this gallery was restored by the French. Traces of gilt can be seen on riders on horses at the beginning of the panel. The lower section of the panel was badly damaged and later filled with cement.

Lower tier: Yama, the Supreme Judge (multiple arms, wields a staff and rides a buffalo), points out to his scribes the upper road representing heaven and the lower one of hell. Departed spirits await judgement. Assistants to Yama shove the wicked through a trap door to the lower regions where torturers deliver punishments such as sawing a body in half for those who overeat. Law breakers have their bones broken. Some of the punished wear iron shackles or have nails pierced through their heads.

Upper tier: A celestial palace is supported by a frieze of Garudas with *apsarās* in the skies.

■ EAST GALLERY
CHURNING OF THE OCEAN OF MILK
This is the most famous panel of bas-reliefs at Angkor Wat and derives from the Indian epic *Bagavata-Pourana*. The Ocean of Milk is churned by gods and demons to generate *amṛta*, the elixir of life. The purpose of the churning is to recover lost treasures such as the source of immortality, Lakṣmī the goddess of good fortune, the milk-white elephant of Indra, and the nymph of loveliness. The retrieval of these objects symbolizes prosperity. It takes place during the second ascent of Viṣṇu, when he is incarnated as a tortoise.

The scene is divided into three tiers. The **lower tier** comprises various aquatic animals, real and mythical, and is bordered by a serpent. The **middle tier** has, on one side, a row of 92 demons (round bulging eyes, crested helmets) and, on the other side, a row of 88 gods (almond-shaped eyes, conical headdresses). They work together by holding and churning the serpent. Hanumān, the monkey god, assists. Viṣṇu, in his reincarnation as a tortoise, offers the back of his shell as a base for the mountain Mandara, and as a pivot for the churning. He sits on the bottom of the Ocean. A huge cord in the form of the body of the serpent Vāsuki acts as a stirring instrument to churn the sea. To begin the motion, the gods and demons twist the serpent's body; the demons hold the head and the gods hold the tail of the serpent. Then by pulling it rhythmically back and forth they cause the pivot to rotate and churn the water. The gods and demons are directed by three persons (identified by their larger size). Indra is on top of Viṣṇu. On the **extreme right** Hanumān, ally of the gods, tickles the serpent. **Upper tier**: During the churning various female spirits emerge.

Viṣṇu appears in this scene again in yet another reincarnation—as a human being—to preside over the 'churning' which, according to legend, lasted more than 1,000 years. Numerous other beings are depicted such as the three-headed elephant mount of Indra, *apsarās* and Lakṣmī, the goddess of beauty. The churning provokes the serpent to vomit the mortal venom which covers the waves. Afraid the venom may destroy the gods and demons, Brahmā intervenes and requests Śiva to devour and drink the venom which will leave an indelible trace on Śiva's throat. He complies and, as a result, the *amṛta* pours forth. The demons rush to capture all the liquid. Viṣṇu hurries to the rescue and assumes yet another reincarnation in the form of Maya, a bewitching beauty, and is able to restore much of the coveted liquid.

INSCRIPTION

Just past the middle of the East Gallery there is an interesting inscription of the early eighteenth century when Angkor Wat was a Buddhist monastery. It tells of a provincial governor who built a small tomb where he deposited the bones of his wife and children. The structure is in poor condition but recognizable in its original location, directly in front of the inscription in the gallery.

VICTORY OF VIṢṆU OVER THE DEMONS

The bas-reliefs in this section of the East Gallery and the south part of the North Gallery were probably completed at a later date, perhaps the fifteenth or sixteenth century. The stiffness of the figures and the cursory workmanship reveal this change. An army of demons marches towards the centre of the panel. **Centre:** Viṣṇu (four arms) sits on the shoulders of a Garuḍa. A scene of carnage follows. Viṣṇu slaughters the enemies on both sides and disperses the bodies. The leaders of the demons (mounted on animals or riding in chariots drawn by monsters) are surrounded by marching soldiers. Another group of warriors (bows and arrows) with their chiefs (in chariots or mounted on huge peacocks) follows.

■ **NORTH GALLERY**

VICTORY OF KRṢṆA OVER BANA THE DEMON KING

At the beginning of the panel Viṣṇu in his incarnation as Kṛṣṇa (framed by two heroes) sits on the shoulders of a Garuḍa. Agni, the God of Fire (multiple arms), sits on a rhinoceros behind him. This scene appears several times. A wall surrounding the city is on fire and prevents the advance of Kṛṣṇa (mounted on a Garuḍa) and his army of gods. This Kṛṣṇa scene also appears several times in the panel. The Garuḍa extinguishes the fire with water from the sacred river Ganges. The demon Bana (multiple arms, mounted on a rhinoceros) approaches from the opposite direction. **Extreme right:** Kṛṣṇa (1,000 heads, hands across his chest) kneels in front of Śiva who sits enthroned on Mount Kailāsa with his wife Pārvatī and their son Gaṇeśa (head of an elephant) as they demand that Śiva spare the life of Bana.

BATTLE BETWEEN THE GODS AND THE DEMONS

A procession of 21 gods of the Brahmānic pantheon march in procession carrying classic attributes and riding traditional mounts. One god battles against a demon while warriors on both sides battle in the background. A series of adversaries follow; then Kubera, God of Riches (with bow and arrow), appears on the shoulders of a *yakṣa;* followed by Skanda, God of War (multiple heads and arms), mounted on a peacock; Indra stands on his mount the elephant; Viṣṇu (four arms) sits on his mount, a Garuḍa; a demon (tiered heads) shaking swords; Yama, God of Death and

Early photograph of the five (two are broken) towers of Angkor Wat from the second causeway at the west entrance

The southwest corner pavilion of the Gallery of Bas-reliefs, c. 1880

Justice (sword and shield), stands in a chariot drawn by oxen; Śiva draws a bow; Brahmā, the Creator, rides his sacred goose; Sūrya, God of the Sun, rides in a chariot pulled by horses; and Varuṇa, God of the Water, stands on a five-headed serpent harnessed like a beast of burden.

■ CORNER PAVILION (NORTHWEST)

Enter the pavilion and walk counter-clockwise (see inset page 97). Several of the scenes are in good condition.

NORTH

A. **Right**: The women's quarters of a palace.
B. **Centre, above the door**: An attempt to abduct Sītā in the forest.
C. **Left, badly damaged**: A scene from the *Rāmāyana*.
   Above: Tiers of monkeys and a pyre.

WEST

D. **Right**: Rāma in his chariot (drawn by geese) returns victorious to Ayodhya.
E. **Centre, above the door**: Rāma and Lakṣmana surrounded by monkeys.
F. **Left**: A conversation between Sītā and Hanumān in the forest; Hanumān gives Rāma's ring to Sītā.
   Below: Superimposed registers of monsters.

SOUTH

G. **Right**: Viṣṇu (seated, four arms) surrounded by *apsarās*.
H. **Centre, above the door**: Rāma and Lakṣmana battle a monster (headless, face on stomach).
I. **Left**: Rāma wins an archery competition; Rāma and Sītā sitting together.

EAST

J. **Right**: Viṣṇu (four arms) on a Garuḍa; Kṛṣṇa (mounted on a Garuḍa) brings back Mount Maniparvata which he took from a demon he killed; his army carries the remains of the demon.
K. **Centre, above the door**: Discussions on an alliance.
   Left: Rāma and his brother Lakṣmana.
   Right: Sugrīva, the monkey king.
L. **Left**: Viṣṇu reclines on the serpent Ananta.
   Above: Apsarās.
   Below: A group of nine gods with their mounts:
   (1) Sūrya in a chariot pulled by horses
   (2) Kubera standing on the shoulders of a *yakṣa*
   (3) Brahmā riding a goose

An illustrator's interpretation of the west entrance (second causeway) to Angkor Wat with a family group in the foreground and monks in the background, 1873

(4) Skanda on a peacock
(5) an unidentified god on a horse
(6) Indra on a three-headed elephant
(7) Yama riding a buffalo
(8) Śiva on a bull
(9) an unidentified god on a lion

■ WEST GALLERY
BATTLE OF LAŃKĀ

This scene, from the *Rāmāyana*, is a long and fierce struggle between Rāma and the demon king Rāvana (10 heads and 20 arms), **near the centre**. It is among the finest of the bas-reliefs at Angkor Wat. The battle takes place in Laṅkā (Sri Lanka) and ends with the defeat of Rāvana, captor of Sītā, the beautiful wife of Rāma. The central figures are the monkey warriors who fight against the *rākṣasas* on Rāma's side. The brutality of war is juxtaposed with a graceful rendition of lithesome monkeys.

Past the centre: Rāma stands on the shoulders of Sugrīva surrounded by arrows; Lakṣmaṇa, his brother, and an old demon, stand by Rāma. Nearby, the demon king Rāvana (10 heads and 20 arms) rides in a chariot drawn by mythical lions. Further on, Nala, the monkey who built Rāma's bridge to Laṅkā, is between them

Rosette motif, frequently seen in Khmer art

leaning on the heads of two lions. He throws the body of one he has just beaten over his shoulder. A monkey prince tears out the tusk of an elephant which is capped with a three-pointed headdress and throws him and the demon to the ground.

Leaving Angkor Wat, 'One looks upon it through misty eyes and with an odd constriction of the throat, for there is only one Angkor. There is no such monument to a vanished people anywhere else in the world'.[19]

---

[19]   R J Casey, *Four Faces of Śiva: The Detective Story of a Vanished Race*, p 59.

Bakheng (Phnom)

It is a testimony to the love of symmetry and balance which evolved its style...in pure simplicity of rectangles its beauty is achieved. It is a pyramid mounting in terraces, five of them....Below Bak-Keng lies all the world of mystery, the world of the Khmer, more mysterious than ever under its cover of impenetrable verdure.[1]

Location: 1,300 metres (4,265 feet) north of Angkor Wat and 400 metres (1,312 feet) south of Angkor Thom

Access: Enter and leave Phnom Bakheng by climbing a long steep path with some steps on the east side of the monument (height 67 metres, 220 feet). In the 1960s this summit was approached by elephant and, according to a French visitor, the ascent was 'a promenade classic and very agreeable'.

Tip: Arrive at the summit just before sunset for a panoramic view of Angkor and its environs. The golden hues of the setting sun on this vista are a memorable sight. When Frenchman Henri Mouhot stood at this point in 1859 he wrote in his diary: 'Steps...lead to the top of the mountain, whence is to be enjoyed a view so beautiful and extensive, that it is not surprising that these people, who have shown so much taste in their buildings, should have chosen it for a site'.[2]

It is possible to see: the five towers of Angkor Wat in the west, Phnom Krom to the southwest near the Grand Lake, Phnom Bok in the northeast, Phnom Kulen in the east, and the West Baray.

Date: Late ninth to early tenth century

King: Yaśovarman I

Religion: Hindu (dedicated to Śiva)

Art Style: Bakheng

BACKGROUND

After Yaśovarman became king in 889, he founded his own capital, Yasoharapura, northwest of Roluos and built Bakheng as his state temple. The site is known today as Angkor and thus Bakheng is sometimes called 'the first Angkor'. A square wall, each side of which is 4 kilometres (2.5 miles) long, surrounded the city. A natural hill in the centre distinguished the site.

---

[1] H Churchill Candee. *Angkor: The Magnificent, The Wonder City of Ancient Cambodia*, pp 217–18.

[2] H Mouhot, *Travels in the Central Parts of Indo-China (Siam), Cambodia, and Laos, During the Years 1858, 1859 and 1860*, 2 vols (John Murray, London, 1864), Vol 1, pp 300–1.

A Day on the Hill of the Gods

This is the most solitary place in all Angkor—and the pleasantest. If it was truly the Mount Meru of the gods, then they chose their habitation well. But if the Khmers had chanced to worship the Greek pantheon instead of that of India, they would surely have built on Phnom Bakheng a temple to Apollo; for it is at sunrise and sunset that you feel its most potent charm. To steal out of the Bungalow an hour before the dawn, and down the road that skirts the faintly glimmering moat of Angkor Wat, before it plunges into the gloom of the forest; and then turn off, feeling your way across the terrace between the guardian lions (who grin amiably at you as you turn the light of your torch upon them); then clamber up the steep buried stairway on the eastern face of the hill, across the plateau and up the five flights of steps, to emerge from the enveloping forest on to the cool high terrace with the stars above you—is a small pilgrimage whose reward is far greater than its cost in effort.

Here at the summit it is very still. The darkness has lost its intensity; and you stand in godlike isolation on the roof of a world that seems to be floating in the sky, among stars peering faintly through wisps of filmy cloud. The dawn comes so unobtrusively that you are unaware of it, until all in a moment you realize that the world is no longer dark. The sanctuaries and altars on the terrace have taken shape about you as if by enchantment; and far below, vaguely as yet, but gathering intensity with every second, the kingdom of the Khmers and the glory thereof spreads out on every side to the very confines of the earth; or so it may well have seemed to the King-God when he visited his sanctuary—how many dawns ago?

Soon, in the east, a faint pale-gold light is diffused above a grey bank of cloud, flat-topped as a cliff, that lies across the far horizon; to which, smooth and unbroken as the surface of a calm sea, stretches the dark ocean of forest, awe-inspiring in its tranquil immensity. To the south the view is the same, save where a long low hill, the shape of a couchant cat, lies in the monotonous sea of foliage like an island. Westward, the pearl-grey waters of the great Baray, over which a thin mist seems to be suspended, turn silver in the growing light, and gleam eerily in their frame of overhanging trees; but beyond them, too, the interminable forest flows on to meet the sky. It is only on the north and north-east that a range of mountains—the

Dangrengs, eighty miles or so away—breaks the contour of the vast, unvarying expanse; and you see in imagination on its eastern rampart the almost inaccessible temple of Prah Vihear.

Immediately below you there is movement. The morning is windless; but one after the other, the tops of the trees growing on the steep sides of the Phnom sway violently to and fro, and a fussy chattering announces that the monkeys have awakened to a new day. Near the bottom of the hill on the south side, threadlike wisps of smoke from invisible native hamlets mingle with patches of mist. And then, as the light strengthens, to the south-east, the tremendous towers of Angkor Wat push their black mass above the grey-green monotony of foliage, and there comes a reflected gleam from a corner of the moat not yet overgrown with weeds. But of the huge city whose walls are almost at your feet, and of all the other great piles scattered far and near over the immense plains that surround you, not a vestige is to be seen. There must surely be enchantment in a forest that knows how to keep such enormous secrets from the all-seeing eye of the sun?

In the afternoon the whole scene is altered. The god-like sense of solitude is the same; but the cool, grey melancholy of early morning has been transformed into a glowing splendour painted in a thousand shades of orange and amber, henna and gold. To the west, the Baray, whose silvery waters in the morning had all the inviting freshness of a Thames backwater, seems now, by some occult process to have grown larger; and spreads, gorgeous but sinister, a sheet of burnished copper, reflecting the fiery glow of the westering sun. Beyond it, the forest, a miracle of colour, flows on to be lost in the splendid conflagration; and to the north and east, where the light is less fierce, you can see that the smooth surface of the sea of tree-tops wears here and there all the tints of an English autumn woodland: a whole gamut of glowing crimson, flaring scarlet, chestnut brown, and brilliant yellow; for even these tropic trees must 'winter'.

By this light you can see, too, what was hidden in the morning: that for a few miles towards the south, the sweep of forest is interrupted by occasional patches of cultivation; ricefields, dry and golden at this season of the year, where cattle and buffaloes are grazing.

...As for the Great Wat, which in the morning had showed itself an indeterminate black mass against the dawn; in this light, and from this place, it is unutterably magical. You have not quite an aerial view—the Phnom is not high enough for that; and even if it were, the ever-encroaching growth of trees on its steep sides shuts out the view of the Wat's whole immense plan. But you can see enough to realize something of the superb audacity of the architects who dared to embark upon a single plan measuring nearly a mile square. Your point of view is diagonal; across the north-west corner of the moat to the soaring lotus-tip of the central sanctuary, you can trace the perfect balance of every faultless line. Worshipful for its beauty, bewildering in its stupendous size, there is no other point from which the Wat appears so inconceivable an undertaking to have been attempted—much less achieved—by human brains and hands.

But however that may be, even while you watch it, the scene is changing under your eyes. The great warm-grey mass in its setting of foliage, turns from grey to gold; then from gold to amber, glowing with ever deeper and deeper warmth as the sun sinks lower. Purple shadows creep upwards from the moat, covering the galleries, blotting out the amber glow; chasing it higher and higher, over the piled up roofs, till it rests for a while on the tiers of carved pinnacles on the highest towers, where an odd one here and there glitters like cut topaz as the level golden rays strike it. The forest takes on colouring that is ever more autumnal; the Baray for ten seconds is a lake of fire; and then, as though the lights had been turned off the pageant is over...and the moon, close to the full, comes into her own, shining down eerily on the scene that has suddenly become so remote and mysterious; while a cool little breeze blows up from the east, and sends the stiff, dry teak-leaves from the trees on the hillside, down through the branches with a metallic rattle.

There is one more change before this nightly transformation-scene is over: a sort of anti-climax often to be seen in these regions. Soon after the sun has disappeared, an after-glow lights up the scene again so warmly as almost to create the illusion that the driver of the sun's chariot has turned his horses, and come back again. Here on Bakheng, the warm tones of sunset return for a few minutes, but faintly, mingling weirdly with the moonlight, to bring into being effects even more elusively lovely than any that have gone before. Then, they too fade; and the moon, supreme at last, shines down unchallenged on the airy temple.

It is lonelier now. After the gorgeous living pageantry of the scene that went before it, the moon's white radiance and the silence are almost unbearably deathlike: far more eerie than the deep darkness of morning with dawn not far behind. With sunset, the companionable chatter of birds and monkeys in the trees below has ceased; they have all gone punctually to bed; even the cicadas for a wonder are silent. Decidedly it is time to go. Five almost perpendicular flights of narrow-treaded steps leading down into depths of darkness are still between you and the plateau on the top of the Phnom: the kind of steps on which a moment of sudden, silly panic may easily mean a broken neck—such is the bathos of such mild adventures. And once on the plateau you can take your choice of crossing it among the crumbled ruins, and plunging down the straight precipitous trace that was once a stairway—or the easy, winding path through the forest round the south side of the hill, worn by the elephants of the explorers and excavators. Either will bring you to where the twin lions sit in the darkness—black now, for here the trees are too dense to let the moonlight through; and so home along the straight road between its high dark walls of forest, where all sorts of humble, half-seen figures flit noiselessly by on their bare feet, with only a creak now and again from the bundles of firewood they carry, to warn you of their passing. Little points of light twinkle out from unseen houses as you pass a hamlet; and, emerging from the forest to the moat-side, the figures of men fishing with immensely long bamboo rods, from the outer wall, are just dimly visible in silhouette against the moonlit water.

H W Ponder, Cambodian Glory, The Mystery of the Deserted Khmer
Cities and their Vanquished Splendour, and a Description of Life
in Cambodia today *(Thornton Butterworth, London, 1936)*

Phnom Bakheng

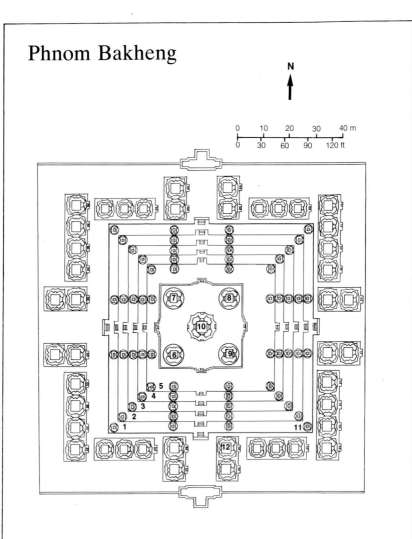

1 first tier of the base
2 second tier
3 third tier
4 fourth tier
5 fifth tier

6–9 towers on the top level
10 Central Sanctuary
11 tower (brick)
12 tower around base

> *It is difficult to believe, at first, that the steep stone cliff ahead of you is, for once, a natural feature of the landscape, and not one of those mountains of masonry to which Angkor so soon accustoms you...the feat of building a flight of wide stone steps up each of its four sides, and a huge temple on the top, is a feat superhuman enough to tax the credulity of the ordinary mortal.[3]*

The temple of Bakheng was cut from rock and faced with sandstone. Traces of this method are visible in the northeast and southeast corners. It reflects improved techniques of construction and the use of more durable materials. This temple is the earliest example of the plan with five sandstone sanctuaries built on the top level of a tiered base arranged like the dots on a die, which became popular later. It is also the first appearance of secondary towers on the tiers of the base.

Symbolism

The number of towers at Bakheng suggests a cosmic symbolism. Originally 109 towers in replica of Mount Meru adorned the temple of Phnom Bakheng but many are missing. The total was made up of five towers on the upper terrace, 12 on each of the five tiers of the base, and another 44 towers around the base. The brick towers on the tiers represent the 12-year cycle of the animal zodiac (**11**). Excluding the Central Sanctuary, there are 108 towers, symbolizing the four lunar phases with 27 days in each phase. The levels (ground, five tiers, upper terrace) number seven and correspond to the seven heavens of Hindu mythology.

Layout

'Every haunted corner of Angkor shares in the general mystery of the Khmers. And here the shadows seem to lie a little deeper, for this hill is like nothing else in the district.'[4]

Phnom Bakheng is square with a base of five tiers (**1–5**) and five sanctuaries (**6–10**) on the top level, occupying the corners and the middle of the terrace. The sides of the base are each 76 metres (249 feet) long and the total height is 13 metres (43 feet). Each side of the base has a steep stairway with a 70° incline. Seated lions flank each side of the steps at each of the five tiers. Vestiges of the wall with entry towers (**12**) surrounding the temple remain.

Seated lions sculpted in the round are on each side of the slope near the summit. The proportions on these lions are particularly fine. Further on, there is a small build-

[3] H W Ponder, *Cambodian Glory: The Mystery of the Deserted Khmer Cities and their Vanquished Splendour...*, p 72.
[4] R J Casey, *Four Faces of Śiva: The Detective Story of a Vanished Race*, p 129.

ing on the right with sandstone pillars; the two *liṅgas* now serve as boundary stones. Continuing towards the top, one comes to a footprint of the Buddha in the centre of the path. This is enclosed in a cement basin and covered with a wooden roof. Closer to the top, remains of an entry tower in the outside wall enclosing the temple are visible. Two sandstone libraries on either side of the walkway are identified by rows of diamond-shaped holes in the walls. Both libraries open to the west and have a porch on the east side.

Small brick sanctuary towers (**11**) occupy the corners of each tier and each side of the stairway.

TOP LEVEL

Five towers are arranged like the dots on a die. The tower in the middle contained the *liṅga*. It is open to all four cardinal points. The other four sanctuaries on the top level also sheltered a *liṅga* on a pedestal and are open on two sides.

The evenly spaced holes in the paving near the east side of the Central Sanctuary probably held wooden posts which supported a roof.

The Central Sanctuary (**10**) is decorated with female divinities under the arches of the corner pillars and *apsarās* with delicately carved bands of foliage above; the pilasters have a raised interlacing of figurines. The *makaras* on the tympanums are lively and strongly executed.

An inscription is visible on the left-hand side of the north door of the Central Sanctuary.

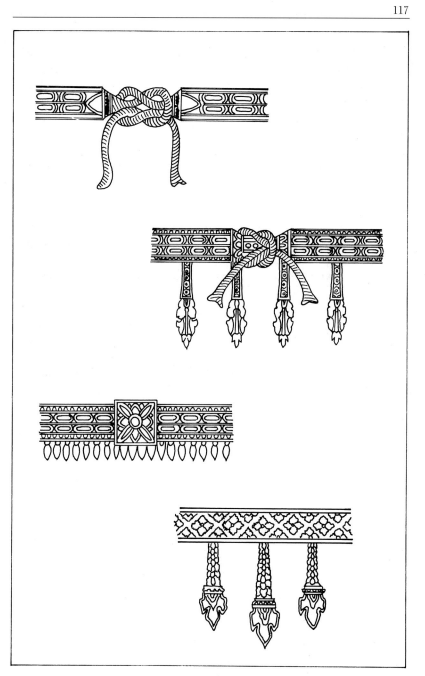

Styles of belts depicted on sculptures at Angkor

Baksei Chamkrong (Prasat):
'the bird who shelters under its wings'

This little temple with its four square tiers of laterite, crowned by a brick sanctuary, might serve for a model in miniature of some of its giant neighbours, and is almost as perfect as the day it was built...[5]

Location: Baksei Chamkrong is located 150 metres (492 feet) north of Phnom Bakheng and 80 metres (262 feet) from the road leading to the south gate of Angkor Thom.

Access: A visit to Baksei Chamkrong can be combined with a stop at the south gate of Angkor Thom. Enter and leave the temple from the east entrance.

Tip: The stairs to the Central Sanctuary are in poor condition but the architecture and decoration of this temple can be viewed by walking around it (in a clockwise direction). Those who persist in climbing to the Central Sanctuary should use the north stairway.

Date: Middle of the tenth century (947)

King: Perhaps begun by Harshavarman I and completed by Rājendravarman II

Religion: Hindu (dedicated to Śiva); may have been a funerary temple for the parents of the king

Art Style: Transitional between Bakheng and Koh Ker

BACKGROUND

According to legend, the king fled during an attack on Angkor and was saved from being caught by the enemy when a large bird swooped down and spread its wings to shelter the king. The name of the temple derives from this legend.

Baksei Chamkrong was the first temple-mountain at Angkor built entirely of durable materials—brick, laterite and sandstone. Even though it is small the balanced proportions and scale of this monument are noteworthy. Inscriptions on the columns of the door and the arches give the date of the temple and mention a golden image of Śiva.

LAYOUT

Baksei Chamkrong is a simple plan with a single tower on top of a square tiered base with four levels of diminishing size (27 metres, 89 feet, a side at the base) built of laterite (**1–4**). The height from the ground to the top of the Central Sanctuary (**7**) is 13 metres (43 feet). Three levels of the base are undecorated but the top one has horizontal moulding around it and serves as a base for the Central Sanctuary. A steep staircase on each side of the base leads to the top.

A brick wall (**5**) with an entry tower (**6**) and sandstone steps enclosed the temple. Although it has almost all disappeared vestiges are visible on the east side of the temple.

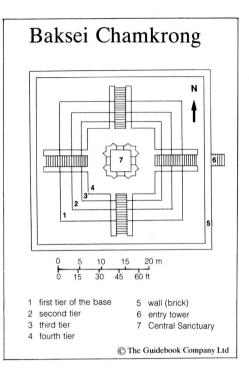

Baksei Chamkrong

| 0 | 5 | 10 | 15 | 20 m |
| 0 | 15 | 30 | 45 | 60 ft |

1	first tier of the base	5	wall (brick)
2	second tier	6	entry tower
3	third tier	7	Central Sanctuary
4	fourth tier		

© The Guidebook Company Ltd

CENTRAL SANCTUARY (7)
The square central tower is built of brick and stands on a sandstone base. It has one door opening to the east with three false doors on the other sides. As is typical of tenth-century Khmer architecture, the columns and lintels are made of sandstone. A vertical panel in the centre of each false door contains motifs of foliage on stems. The interior of the tower has a sunken floor and a vault with a corbel arch.

The finely worked decoration on the sandstone columns and horizontal beams above the doors imitates wood carving. An outline of female divinities can be seen in the bricks at the corners of the tower. A three-headed elephant on the east lintel is finely carved.

[5] H W Ponder, *Cambodian Glory: The Mystery of the Deserted Khmer Cities and their Vanished Splendour...* , p 42.

Banteay Kdei

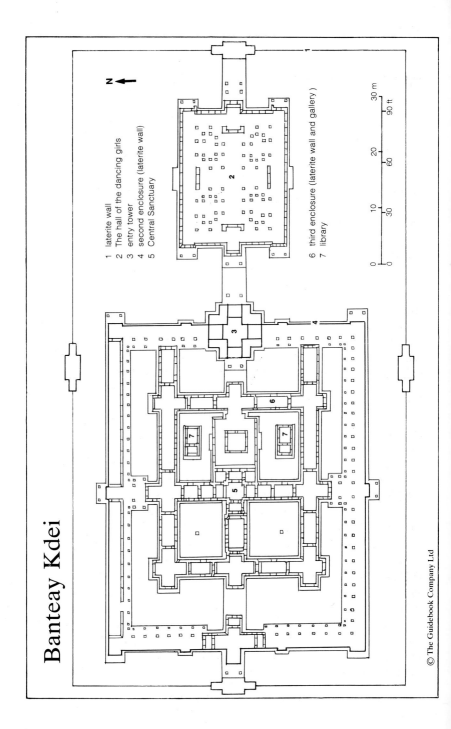

N ←

1 laterite wall
2 The hall of the dancing girls
3 entry tower
4 second enclosure (laterite wall)
5 Central Sanctuary

6 third enclosure (laterite wall and gallery)
7 library

0	10	20	30 m
0	30	60	90 ft

© The Guidebook Company Ltd

Banteay Kdei: 'the citadel of the cells'

*In the ruin and confusion of Banteay Kdei the carvings take one's interest.
They are piquant, exquisite, not too frequent...they seem meant...to make
adorable a human habitation.*[6]

Location: Banteay Kdei is located south of Ta Prohm

Access: Enter the monument from the east and leave at the west or vice versa;
               either way, also visit Srah Srang.

Date: Middle of the 12th century to the beginning of the 13th century

King: Jayavarman VII

Religion: Mahāyāna Buddhism

Art Style: At least two different art periods—Angkor Wat and Bayon—are discernible
               at Banteay Kdei.

BACKGROUND

Banteay Kdei has not been restored and allows the visitor to experience what it may
have looked like originally. Changes and additions account for its unbalanced layout.
Banteay Kdei was built of soft sandstone and many of the galleries and porches have
collapsed. The wall enclosing the temple was built of reused stones.

LAYOUT

The temple is built on the ground level for use as a Buddhist monastery. The elements of the original design of Banteay Kdei seem to have been a Central Sanctuary
(**5**), a surrounding gallery (**6**) and a passageway connected to another gallery. A moat
enclosed the original features of the temple. Another enclosure and two libraries were
among the additions in the Bayon period. The outer enclosure (700 by 500 metres,
2,297 by 1,640 feet) is made of laterite (**1**) and has four entry towers.

A rectangular courtyard to the east is known as 'the hall of the dancing girls', a
name derived from the decoration which includes dancers (**2**).

The entry tower of the second enclosure (**3**) is in the shape of a cross with three
passages; the two on either end are connected to the laterite wall of the enclosure (**4**)
(320 by 200 metres, 1,050 by 656 feet). The inner walls of the enclosure are decorated with scrolls of figures and large female divinities in niches. In the interior court
there is a frieze of Buddhas.

A causeway of a later date, bordered with serpents, leads to the entry tower of the
third enclosure. It comprises a laterite wall (**6**) and includes a gallery with a double
row of sandstone pillars that open onto a courtyard. **Tip**: Parts of this area have been
walled in and passage is limited.

---

[6]   H Churchill Candee, *Angkor: The Magnificent, The Wonder City of Ancient Cambodia*, pp 249–50.

Vestiges of the wooden ceiling can still be seen in the Central Sanctuary. The galleries and halls, which join it in a cross to the four entry towers, are probably additions. Two libraries (7) open to the west in the courtyards on the left and right of the causeway.

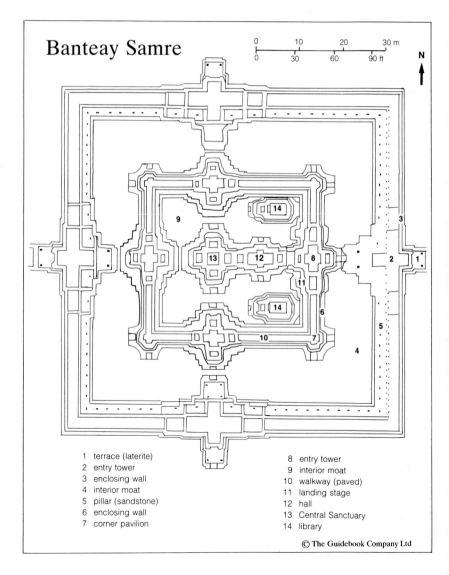

Banteay Samre

0   10   20   30 m

0   30   60   90 ft

N

1 terrace (laterite)	8 entry tower
2 entry tower	9 interior moat
3 enclosing wall	10 walkway (paved)
4 interior moat	11 landing stage
5 pillar (sandstone)	12 hall
6 enclosing wall	13 Central Sanctuary
7 corner pavilion	14 library

© The Guidebook Company Ltd

Banteay Samre: 'the citadel of the Samre'

Location: 400 metres (1,312 feet) east of the East Baray
Access: A visit to Banteay Samre can be combined with a trip to Banteay Srei. Enter at the east and leave by the south entrance.
Date: Toward the middle of the 12th century
King: Sūryavarman II
Religion: Hindu (dedicated to Viṣṇu)
Art Style: Angkor Wat

BACKGROUND
The name 'Samre' refers to an ethnic group of people who come from the region at the base of Phnom Kulen. Although no inscription has been found for this temple, the style is of the 'classic' art of the middle period like that of Angkor Wat and the monument most likely dates from the same period, or perhaps slightly later. The proportions of Banteay Samre are splendid. Unique features are an interior moat with laterite paving, which must have given an ethereal atmosphere to the temple, and the use of stone finials across the central ridge of the roof. All of the buildings around the moat are on a raised base with horizontal moulding, decorated in some areas with figures framed by lotus buds.

Banteay Samre is one of the most complete complexes at Angkor as the French spent eight years restoring this monument using the method of anastylosis (see glossary page 230). Unfortunately the absence of maintenance over the past 20 years is evident.

LAYOUT
The plan of Banteay Samre is approximately square and consists of a surrounding wall, an enclosure of galleries with an entry tower on each side, a courtyard and a Central Sanctuary opening to the east, which is approached by a long hall with a library on each side.

Enter from the east along a causeway (length 200 metres, 656 feet) paved in laterite which leads to the east entry tower of the wall enclosing the monument. The causeway, on two levels, which is not shown on the plan, is bordered on each side by serpent balustrades in the style of Angkor Wat (only vestiges remain). The end of the causeway leads to a stairway flanked by crouching lions on short columns. The retaining wall along this causeway bears fine quality decoration. The laterite foundations of two stairways are visible. This long and dramatic causeway was probably covered with a wooden roof.

Serpent balustrade with multi-heads spread in the shape of a fan

© The Guidebook Company Ltd

The small size, unimpressive form and Bayon art style of this entry tower (2) at the east suggest it is not the original one but built later than the monument. Next there is a laterite terrace (1), also built later, that leads to and forms the base of the entry tower of the enclosure (3) shown on the plan (83 by 77 metres, 272 by 92 feet). There is an interior moat (4) surrounded by a false porch with sandstone pillars (5). This aisle was covered in curved tiles and vestiges of the framework are still visible in the wall. A gallery follows with windows decorated with five to seven balusters on the south side. The other three entry towers on the west, north and south of the gallery were similar—built of laterite and sandstone in the shape of a cross with a wing on each side connecting to the galleries, and with two porches and pillars.

The next enclosure (44 by 38 metres, 144 by 125 feet) is raised above the surface and consists of a low narrow laterite gallery (6). It has a pavilion (7) in each corner and an entry tower with a ridged crest in the middle of each side (8). These structures, which were probably added at a later date, have only one door, which opens on to the interior moat (9), and windows with balusters that have been walled up. There are stone finials across the centre ridge of the roof of the galleries.

A sandstone paved walkway surrounds the moat (10). Stairs leading to the moat are bordered by serpent balustrades terminating with a remarkably finely carved fan of multiple heads. These so-called 'landing stages' (11) intercept the walkway around the courtyard.

The entry tower on the east of the second enclosure leads to an open-air platform and a long hall (12) in front of the Central Sanctuary (13). It consists of another entry tower with a stairway on each side.

CENTRAL SANCTUARY (13)
This has a porch with a double pediment on each side opening to the cardinal points

and three false doors. The upper part of the sanctuary has four recessed tiers and terminates in a top with a profile shaped like a lotus bud. The reliefs on the upper levels of this Hindu sanctuary depict Buddhist scenes.

LIBRARIES

The cramped placement of the libraries (**14**) on the left and right sides of the long hall preceding the Central Sanctury suggests a change of mind in the original plan. The libraries have slender proportions with cylindrical vaulting, false aisles, a false attic pierced with long windows, and pediments. The decoration on the false doors is remarkably fine.

   Tip: To see the decoration on the highest part of the Central Sanctuary walk straight through to the end; then, go either to the left or the right on the sandstone walkway and look back at the Central Sanctuary.

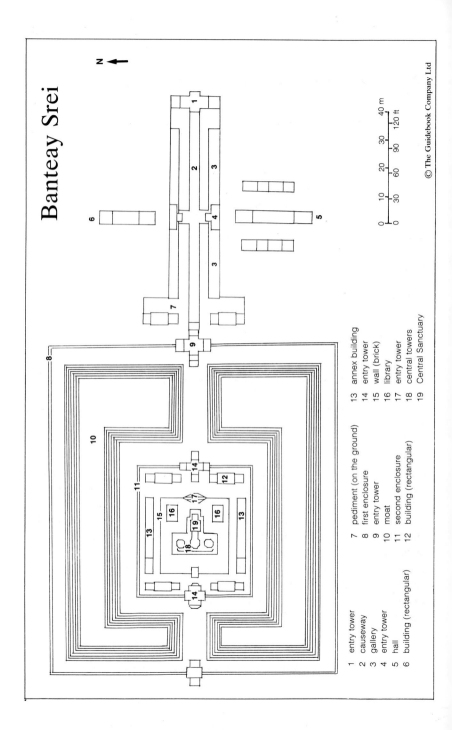

Banteay Srei

N

1	entry tower	7 pediment (on the ground)	13 annex building
2	causeway	8 first enclosure	14 entry tower
3	gallery	9 entry tower	15 wall (brick)
4	entry tower	10 moat	16 library
5	hall	11 second enclosure	17 entry tower
6	building (rectangular)	12 building (rectangular)	18 central towers
		19 Central Sanctuary

0   10   20   30   40 m
0   30   60   90   120 ft

Banteay Srei: 'the citadel of the women'

Banteai Srei, the 'citadel of women'...is an exquisite miniature; a fairy palace in the heart of an immense and mysterious forest; the very thing that Grimm delighted to imagine, and that every child's heart has yearned after, but which maturer years has sadly proved too lovely to be true. And here it is, in the Cambodian forest at Banteai Srei, carved not out of the stuff that dreams are made of, but of solid sandstone.[7]

Location: Banteay Srei is 25 kilometres (15.5 miles) northeast of the Bayon
Access: Enter and leave the temple by the east entrance
Date: Second half of the tenth century (967)
King: Reigns of Rājendravarman II and Jayavarman V
Religion: Hindu (dedicated to Śiva)
Art Style: Banteay Srei

BACKGROUND

The enchanting temple of Banteay Srei is nearly everyone's favourite site. The special charm of this small temple lies in its remarkable state of preservation, small size and excellence of decoration. The unanimous opinion amongst the French archaeologists who worked at Angkor is that Banteay Srei is a 'precious gem' and a 'jewel in Khmer art'.

Banteay Srei was built by a Brahman who was the grandson of Harshavarman II and some describe it as being closer in architecture and decoration to Indian models than any other temple at Angkor. A special feature of the exquisite decoration was the use of a hard pink sandstone which enabled the 'technique of sandalwood carving with even an Indian scent to it'.

Architectural and decorative features of Banteay Srei are unique and exceptionally fine. A tapestry-like background of foliage covers the walls of the structures in the central group as if a deliberate attempt had been made to leave no space undecorated. The architecture is distinguished by superimposed pediments, terminal motifs on the frames of the arches, and standing figures in the niches. Panels are decorated with scenes inspired by Indian epics especially the *Rāmāyana* and its execution has a liveliness not seen in the more formal decoration of earlier temples.

---

[7]   H W Ponder, *Cambodian Glory: The Mystery of the Deserted Khmer Cities and their Vanquished Splendour...*, p 254.

The temple was discovered by the French in 1914 but the site was not cleared until 1924. The theft of several important pieces of sculpture and lintels by a Westerner in 1923 hastened the archaeological work. The thief was arrested and imprisoned in Phnom Penh. He was released after the return of the stolen pieces.

Popular decorative motif at Banteay Srei with a mask-like kāla in the centre whose claws support the heads of mythical lions on each side

Banteay Srei is the first temple at Angkor to have been completely restored by the process of anastylosis (see glossary page 230), after the French studied the method at Borobudur in Java.

Tip: Do not be surprised by the smallness of this temple. The quality of architecture and decoration make up for any shortcomings in size. As M Glaize wrote, Banteay Srei is 'a sort of "caprice" where the detail, of an abundance and incomparable prettiness, sweeps away the mass'.[8]

The inscription relating the foundation of the temple was found in the entry tower of the outer enclosure in 1936.

LAYOUT

'For just the sensation of coming into Banteai Srei is something beyond ordinary experience.'[9] Banteay Srei is square in plan, surrounded by a laterite wall with vestibules on the east and west. The temple is enclosed by three walls.

The **east entrance** (1) is a laterite entry tower in the shape of a cross with a door on each side. The sandstone pillars and a pediment depicting Indra on a three-headed elephant on the east porch of the tower give a hint of the warm colour of the stone and the exquisite decoration to come.

A **long causeway** (2) with decorative sandstone markers leads to the wall surrounding the temple. On either side of the causeway are galleries (3) with laterite walls and sandstone pillars, in the middle of which are small entry towers (4). To the left are three long parallel halls (oriented north to south) (5) and to the right is a single building (6) with a superb pediment of Viṣṇu in his *avatāras* as man-lion. He holds the demon king down and claws his chest.

At the end of the causeway on the right is a pediment lying on the ground (7) depicting the abduction of Sītā, wife of Rāma.

The first enclosure (8) consists of a moat (10) with laterite tiers and ditches on each side and a cross-shaped entry tower (9). The second enclosure also has a laterite wall (11) with entry towers at the east and west (14). The area inside includes six laterite annex buildings—two each on the east and west (12) and a long one on the north and south (13)—which may have been rest houses used for meditation. The entry tower at the east of this enclosure is in the shape of a cross with two porches and triangular-shaped pediments reminiscent of wooden architecture and framed with large terminal scrolls. Inscriptions can be seen on the door frames of this tower. A brick wall surrounds the central area (15). In the courtyard there are libraries (16) on the left and right sides of the entrance (17) which open to the west. The walls are of laterite and sandstone with a corbel vault of brick.

CENTRAL GROUP

The central group of structures at Banteay Srei comprises three towers arranged side by side on a common low platform (18). Each tower has four recessed storeys decorated with miniature replicas of the main tower which symbolize the dwelling of the gods. The towers are guarded by mythical figures with human torsos and animal heads kneeling at the base of the stairs leading to the entrances. Some of these sculpted figures are copies; the originals are preserved in the National Museum at Phnom Penh. A comparison can be made at the east of the central group in front of the right tower. The figure on the right is geniune whereas the one on the left is a copy.

Divinities on the central towers: The figures of male and female divinities in the niches of the corners are perfect in proportion, balance and artistic style. The females have plaited hair or a bun tied at the side in a style characteristic of Banteay Srei, simple dress, heavy earrings that weigh down their ear lobes, and garlands of pearls that hang from their belts. Their skirts are loosely draped. The figures are separated from the head of *kāla* (above the door) by a lotus; musicians playing cymbals provide the rhythm for the steps of a dancer with a large bell skirt.

Library on the left (south): On the east pediment the giant Rāvaṇa (multiple heads and arms) shakes Mount Kailāsa, represented by a pyramid on a background of

8   M Glaize, *Les Monuments du Groupe d'Angkor: Guide*, p 230.
9   S Sitwell, *The Red Chapels of Banteai Srei: And Temples in Cambodia, India, Siam and Nepal* (Weidenfeld & Nicolson, London, 1962), p 70.

stylized forest. Śiva sits on his throne at the summit of the mountain while his wife, Pārvatī, cuddles up to him. Rāvaṇa wants to attract Śiva's attention and shakes Mount Kailāsa with all his might. The creatures, hermits and animals who live on the mountain express their terror and flee to the jungle. On the first step the monkey-faced guardian of the mountain raises his hand, perhaps to warn Rāvaṇa that one day he will be destroyed by the monkeys. At the summit, Śiva prepares to bring the whole weight of the mountain upon Rāvaṇa while Pārvatī clings to his shoulder in terror.

On the west pediment: Kāma, God of Love (on the left), shoots an arrow at Śiva who sits on top of Mount Kailāsa; his wife Pārvatī is beside him and hands a rosary to Śiva to try to distract him in his meditation. A group of ascetics below Śiva and guardians with human bodies and animal heads complete the scene.

Library on the right (north): On the east pediment (from the top) Indra, God of the Sky, is depicted scattering celestial rain (parallel rows of oblique lines) on a stylized forest inhabited by animals. Indra rides in a chariot drawn by a three-headed elephant and is surrounded by winds and clouds (wavy lines). A serpent rises in the midst of the rain. Kṛṣṇa, as a baby, and his brother, Balarāma (holding the shaft of a plough), pass by.

On the west pediment the theme concerns Kṛṣṇa who murders his cruel uncle, King Kamsa, because he tried to kill him when he was a child. Kṛṣṇa clutches Kamsa by the hair. The venue is a palace of two storeys on columns which is a fine example of the architecture of the period. Garlands decorate the first floor and the profile of the palace is a series of recessed tiers. The two main figures in the scene are indicated by their size.

Central Sanctuary (19): The guardians in the corners of the central tower are magnificent specimens of Khmer sculpture. Their hair is swept up in a cylindrical chignon and they hold a lotus bud in one hand and a lance in the other.

Lintels: North shows the battle between the monkeys, Vali and Sugrīva; west, the abduction of Sītā.

Male divinity in niche supported by mythical beings with monkey faces, Banteay Srei

Baphuon

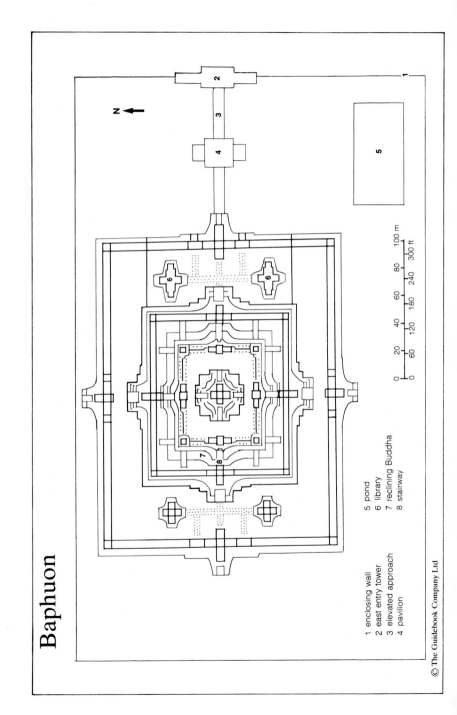

1 enclosing wall
2 east entry tower
3 elevated approach
4 pavilion
5 pond
6 library
7 reclining Buddha
8 stairway

N

0   20   40   60   80   100 m
0   60   120 180 240 300 ft

Baphuon

North of the Golden Tower [Bayon]...rises the Tower of Bronze [Baphuon],
higher even than the Golden Tower: a truly astonishing spectacle, with
more than ten chambers at its base.[1]

Location: Baphuon is located 200 metres (656 feet) northwest of the Bayon and
south of Phimeanakas.

Access: Enter and leave at the east.

Tip: Access to the summit is difficult as much of the temple has collapsed and it
is overgrown but for those stalwarts who want to go to the top, use the
west stairway. At the summit one can enjoy a bird's-eye view of the causeway with columns at the east and the temple of Phimeanakas on the
left. Visitors should walk down the causeway, climb the steps to the first
tier, turn left and walk around the temple, always keeping it on their right.

Date: Middle of the 11th century (1060)

King: Udayadityavarman II

Religion: Hindu (dedicated to Śiva)

Art Style: Baphuon

BACKGROUND

The grandeur of Baphuon as described above by Zhou Daguan is unrecognizable
today because of the poor condition of the temple. The French were in the process of
restoring this temple when they were forced to leave Angkor in 1972 because of war.
Baphuon is situated inside the royal city of Angkor Thom but dates from the eleventh
century and was built before the city was established. An interesting feature of Baphuon are the bas-reliefs which are scenes carved in small squares. Unfortunately few
of these are visible because of the poor state of the temple. The narrative themes are
realistic depictions of daily life and forest scenes.

LAYOUT

Baphuon is a single sanctuary temple-mountain situated on a high base. It is a symbolical representation of Mount Meru. A rectangular sandstone wall measuring 425
by 125 metres (1,394 by 410 feet) encloses the temple (1). A long sandstone elevated
approach (200 metres, 656 feet) at the east entrance (3) forms a bridge to the main
temple. It is supported by three rows of short columns. **Tip:** Before walking down the

---

[1]   Chou Ta-Kuan (Zhou Daguan), *The Customs of Cambodia*, p 2.

Early photograph of the Bayon. The columns in the foreground originally supported a roof

approach turn left at the east entry tower (**2**) and walk to the end of the gallery for a superb view of a four-faced tower of the Bayon framed by a doorway of Baphuon. The approach is intercepted by a pavilion in the shape of a cross (**4**) with terraces on the left and right sides. Turn left and walk to the opening in the second window for a fine view of the arrangement of the imposing pillars under the approach. Continue to the end of the gallery to see a rectangular paved pool (**5**).

The temple stands on a rectangular sandstone base with five levels that are approximately the same size, rather than the more common form of successively smaller levels. The first, second and third levels are surrounded by sandstone galleries. Baphuon is the first structure in which stone galleries with a central tower appear. Two libraries (**6**) in the shape of a cross with four porches stand in the courtyard. They were originally connected by an elevated walkway supported by columns.

The gallery of the enclosure collapsed and, at a later date, the stones from it were modelled into the shape of a reclining Buddha (**7**) that spans the length of the west wall (the head is on the left, facing the temple). It is an abstract form and the outline of this Buddha is difficult to distinguish. A stairway (**8**) leading to the summit begins in the middle of the Buddha.

The top level is in poor condition due to several collapses. Originally there was a Central Sanctuary with two wings. Each side of the entrance to the Central Sanctuary is carved with fine animated figures. If you look carefully you can see these from the ground on the west side.

Tip: The view from the top with Phnom Bakheng in the south and Phimeanakas in the north is magnificent.

Bayon

We stand before it stunned. It is like nothing else in the land.[2]

Location: The Bayon is located in the centre of the city of Angkor Thom, 1,500
metres (4,921 feet) from the south gate.
Access: Enter the Bayon from the east
Date: Late 12th century to early 13th century
King: Jayavarman VII
Religion: Buddhist
Art Style: Bayon

BACKGROUND

The Bayon vies with Angkor Wat as the favourite monument of visitors. The two
evoke similar aesthetic responses yet are different in purpose, design, architecture
and decoration. The dense jungle surrounding the temple camouflaged its position in
relation to other structures at Angkor so it was not known for some time that the
Bayon stands in the exact centre of the city of Angkor Thom. Even after this was
known, the Bayon was erroneously connected with the city of Yaśovarman I and thus
dated to the ninth century. A pediment found in 1925 depicting an Avalokiteśvara
identified the Bayon as a Buddhist temple. This discovery moved the date of the monument ahead some 300 years to the late twelfth century. Even though the date is
firmly implanted and supported by archaeological evidence, the Bayon remains one of
the most enigmatic temples of the Angkor group. Its symbolism, original form and
subsequent changes and constructions have not yet been untangled.

The Bayon was built nearly 100 years after Angkor Wat. The basic structure and
earliest part of the temple are not known. Since it was located at the centre of a royal
city it seems possible that the Bayon would have originally been a temple-mountain
conforming to the symbolism of a microcosm of Mount Meru. The middle part of the
temple was extended during the second phase of building. The Bayon of today be-
longs to the third and last phase of the art style.

The architectural scale and composition of the Bayon exude grandness in every
aspect. Its elements juxtapose each other to create balance and harmony. Over 200
large faces carved on the 54 towers give this temple its majestic character. The faces
with slightly curving lips, eyes placed in shadow by the lowered lids utter not a word
and yet force you to guess much', wrote P Jennerat de Beerski in the 1920s.[3] It is

[2] H Churchill Candee, *Angkor: The Magnificent, The Wonder City of Ancient Cambodia*, p 126.
[3] P J de Beerski, *Angkor: Ruins in Cambodia*, p 124.

(following pages) *The Bayon before being cleared,* c. 1875

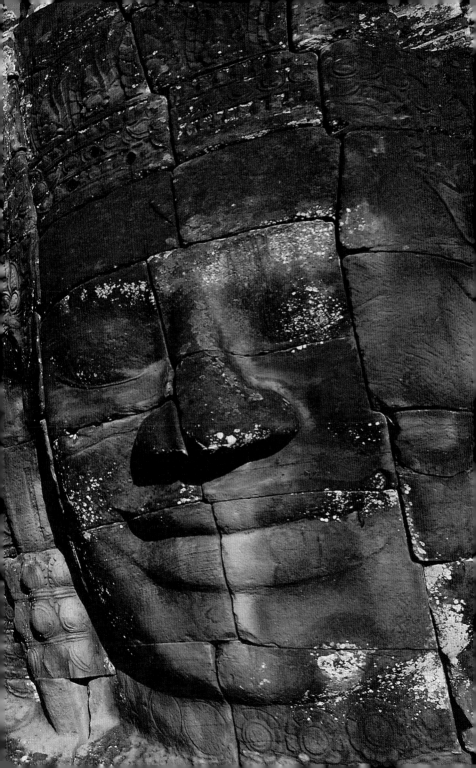

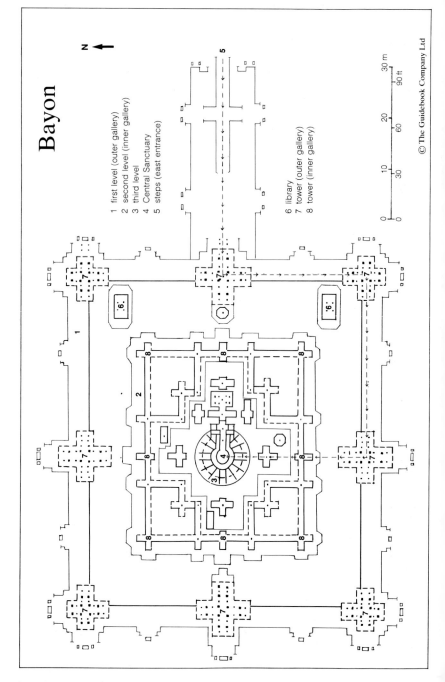

Bayon

1 first level (outer gallery)
2 second level (inner gallery)
3 third level
4 Central Sanctuary
5 steps (east entrance)

6 library
7 tower (outer gallery)
8 tower (inner gallery)

(preceding pages) *One of over two hundred faces at the Bayon*

generally accepted that the four faces on each of the towers are images of the bo-dhisattva Avalokiteśvara and that they signify the omnipresence of the king. The characteristics of these faces—a broad forehead, downcast eyes, wide nostrils, thick lips that curl upwards slightly at the ends—combine to reflect the famous 'smile of Angkor'.

LAYOUT

A peculiarity of the Bayon is the absence of an enclosing wall. It is, though, protected by the wall surrounding the city of Angkor Thom. The basic plan of the Bayon is a simple one comprising three levels (1–3). The first and second levels are square galleries featuring bas-reliefs. A circular **Central Sanctuary** (4) dominates the third level. Despite this seemingly simple plan, the arrangement of the Bayon is complex, with a maze of galleries, passages and steps connected in a way that makes the levels practically indistinguishable and creates dim lighting, narrow walkways, and low ceilings.

Enter the Bayon from the east (5) at the steps leading to a terrace. The exterior of the Bayon, the one a visitor first encounters, is a square gallery on the ground or first level (1). This gallery is interspersed with eight entry towers (7)—one in each corner and one in the middle of each side. All of these eight structures are in the shape of a cross. The gallery was probably originally covered with a roof, perhaps of wood.

Tip: For those who have limited time, enter the Bayon at the east, turn left at the first gallery and follow the arrows marked on the plan.

The decoration on the pillars in front of the entry tower at the east is character-istic of the Bayon style and is exceptionally beautiful. It is the recurring theme of the *apsarās* but with a different treatment. A typical composition is a group of three *apsarās* dancing on a bed of lotuses. They are in a triangular formation. The figure in the centre is larger than those on either side. A plain background highlights both the dancers and the intricately carved frame comprising a lightly etched pattern of flow-ers and leaves that looks like tapestry. (Although a group of three dancers is typical, similar scenes are made up of only one or two dancers.) **Tip**: The absence of a roof on these pillars allows sufficient light for the visitor to view and photograph this motif at all times of the day.

The two galleries of bas-reliefs are distinguished by the degree of elevation. The first or outer gallery is all on one level whereas the second or inner gallery is on dif-ferent levels and the passage is sometimes difficult. The layout of the inner gallery can be misleading but as long as the reliefs are in view you are still in the second gallery.

On the interior of the first level there are two libraries (6), one on each side near the corners at the east side of the gallery.

The second gallery of bas-reliefs has a tower in each corner and another one on each side which combines to form an entry tower (8).

On the interior of the second level there is a unit of galleries at each corner that form a cross with indentations. Each corner has a tower and a courtyard. A high terrace parallels the profile of the cross-shaped gallery.

A face of the Bayon enshrouded with vegetation on an old banknote

The architectural climax is the third level (3), with the Central Sanctuary and the faces of Avalokiteśvara. The east side of this area is crammed with a series of small rooms and entry towers. The multitude of faces at different levels affords endless fascination. 'Godliness in the majesty and the size; mystery in the expression', wrote de Beerski when he looked at the faces in the 1920s.[4]

The central mass is circular, a shape that is uncommon in Khmer art. Small porches with pediments provide the bases for the monumental faces while windows with balusters keep the diffusion of light to a minimum. The faces on the four sides of the eight towers marking the cardinal directions are exceptionally dramatic depictions.

The interior of the Central Sanctuary is a cell and is surrounded by a narrow passage. The summit of the central mass is undoubtedly the 'Golden Tower' which Zhou Daguan said marked the centre of the kingdom and was 'flanked by more than twenty lesser towers and several hundred stone chambers'.[5]

THE GALLERY OF BAS-RELIEFS

'They have homely human things to tell and they tell them without affectation', wrote H Churchill Candee of the bas-reliefs in the galleries of the Bayon.[6]

Tip: View the galleries of bas-reliefs clockwise, always keeping the monument on the right. Do not get so absorbed with the reliefs that you forget to stop at each opening and enjoy the view of the faces on the third level.

The bas-reliefs at the Bayon consist of two galleries. The inner one is decorated with mythical scenes. The bas-reliefs on the outer gallery are a marked departure from anything previously seen at Angkor. They contain genre scenes of everyday life—markets, fishing, festivals with cockfights and jugglers and so on—and historical scenes with battles and processions. The reliefs are more deeply carved than at Angkor Wat but the representation is less stylized. The scenes are presented mostly in two or three horizontal panels. The lower one shows no awareness of the laws of perspective whereas the upper tier presents scenes of the horizon. They exhibit a wealth of creativity, balanced compositions and curious attempts at achieving perspective.

Descriptions of the bas-reliefs in this guidebook follow the normal route for viewing the Bayon. They begin in the middle of the East Gallery and continue clockwise. The other (northern) side of the East Gallery, therefore, is described at the end of the section. Identifying characteristics are in parenthesis and the locations and scenes on the bas-reliefs are in bold type.

THE OUTER OR FIRST LEVEL
The outer gallery of bas-reliefs was probably open to all worshippers of Buddhism. The depictions may have served as a teaching vehicle to disseminate the tenets of Buddhism. Some of the scenes in this gallery are incomplete. For evidence of this, look at the extremities such as the corners, particularly near the top of the wall.

■ EAST GALLERY
The workmanship of the reliefs in this gallery is excellent. They are divided into three panels and depict a military procession with banners and a background of gum and fig trees (1). On the top tier, warriors (short hair and no head covering) are armed with javelins and shields while those on the lower tier have goatees and wear exotic headdresses suggesting they are Chinese. Musicians accompany the warriors. Horsemen riding bareback flank the musicians. The commanders of the troops, including Jayavarman VII, identified by umbrellas with tiers and insignias, are mounted on elephants. Cavalry precede and women of the palace follow the king. Towards the end of the procession, covered wooden carts (on the lower tier) of the same style as are used today, carry provisions of food for the military. A crouching woman blows a fire for a cooking pot. Looking through the doorway between (1) and (2) one can see the south library.

The military procession continues (2). The reliefs follow on with genre scenes of everyday life and include a coconut tree with monkeys. A tiered wooden building with people suggests either a shop or a restaurant. The headdresses, clothing and objects hanging from the ceiling suggest that the people inside the building are Chinese.

4   P J de Beerski, *Angkor: Ruins in Cambodia*, p 125.

5   Chou Ta-Kuan (Zhou Daguan), *The Customs of Cambodia*, p 2.

6   H Churchill Candee, *Angkor: The Magnificent, The Wonder City of Ancient Cambodia*, p 139.

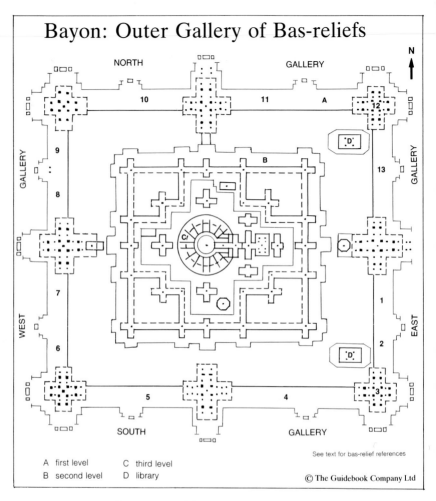

Bayon: Outer Gallery of Bas-reliefs

NORTH   GALLERY   N

10   11   A   12

9

8   B   13

C

7   1

WEST   EAST

6   2

5   4   3

SOUTH   GALLERY

See text for bas-relief references

A first level   C third level
B second level   D library

© The Guidebook Company Ltd

■ CORNER PAVILION (SOUTHEAST) (3)

The carving in this area is unfinished. Identifiable scenes include a wooden palace with a superb *kendi* (drinking vessel) underneath the stairs of the two storeys. Nearby a Buddha has been altered to represent a *linga*, after the temple became Hindu under a later king. An ingenious depiction of a boat spans a 90-degree turn in the wall.

■ SOUTH GALLERY

The scenes in the first part of this gallery (4) contain some of the finest workmanship of all the reliefs at the Bayon. The panel begins with a historical scene depicting the naval battle of 1177 between the Khmers (with no head covering) and the Chams, their neighbouring enemies from southeast Vietnam. The Chams are readily identifiable by their hats which resemble an upside-down lotus. The boats are majestically portrayed with richly ornamented prows and a galley with the rowers and warriors armed with javelins, bows, and shields. Helen Churchill Candee must have had these boats in mind when she wrote: 'One wonders if Cleopatra floated in greater elegance'.[7] Action is provided by corpses being thrown overboard and sometimes being eaten by crocodiles.

On the lower row, genre scenes of daily life along the shores of the Great Lake are depicted with spirit and candour—a woman removing lice from another one's hair, a mother playing with her children, another woman kneeling with her arms around a figure who is writhing in pain, which may be a scene of childbirth assisted by a midwife, and a patient in a hospital. A hunter prepares his bow to shoot a large animal. A fishing scene follows: people on board one of the boats play a board game; a scene of a cockfight; above, fishermen on Tonle Sap Lake and below, women fishmongers. Scenes of the palace follow—princesses surrounded by their suitors, wrestlers, sword fighters, chess players and a fight between wild boars. An outline of a giant figure, perhaps the king, surmounts this entire scene.

Further along the gallery, the battle resumes. (**Lower tier**), the Chams arrive in boats and disembark. (**Upper tier**), the battle continues on land with the Khmers, disguised as giants (closely-cropped hair and cords around their torsos) winning. Afterwards, the king sits in his palace amidst his subjects celebrating their victory. Carpenters cut sandstone, blacksmiths pound iron, and cooks tend fires in preparation for a celebration.

In the second part of the South Gallery (5) only the lower tier is finished. The scene is a military procession and the main point of interest is the weapons of war used by the Khmers such as a large cross-bow mounted on the back of an elephant manned by archers and a catapult mounted on wheels.

■ WEST GALLERY

Many reliefs in this gallery (6) are unfinished. (**Lower tier**), warriors and their chiefs, mounted on elephants, pass through mountains and forests (identified by small triangles); (**near the centre**), an ascetic scales a tree to escape an attack by a tiger; (**above**), scenes depict the methods used for constructing temples such as grinding and polishing sandstone.

(**Beyond the door**), a so-called 'Civil War' (7): This appears to be a street scene with crowds of men and women threatening others armed and ready for battle. The mêlée continues with hordes of warriors and elephants participating in the action.

---

[7]   H Churchill Candee, *Angkor: The Magnificent, The Wonder City of Ancient Cambodia*, p 141.

'My Cambodian guide is insistent that we should depart. We have no lanterns, he
tells me, on our carts, and it behoves us to return before the hour of the tiger.

   Before I leave, however, I raise my eyes to look at the towers which overhang me,
drowned in verdure, and I shudder suddenly with an indefinable fear as I perceive,
falling upon me from above, a huge, fixed smile; and then another smile again,
beyond, on another stretch of wall,…and then three, and then five, and then ten.
They appear everywhere, and I realise that I have been overlooked from all sides
by the faces of the quadrupled-visaged towers. I had forgotten them, although I had
been advised of their existence. They are of a size, these masks carved in the air, so
far exceeding human proportions that it requires a moment or two fully to
comprehend them.'

   Pierre Loti, Siam, W P Baines, trans (T Werner Laurie, London, n d, c 1902)

In the second part of the West Gallery (**8**) is a scene of hand-to-hand combat in
which warriors armed with clubs harass others who protect themselves with shields.
A fish swallows a deer on the lower register. An inscription, incised under a shrimp,
says that 'the king follows those vanquished in hiding'.
(**Beyond the door**), (**9**) a peaceful procession against a background of trees depicts
the king (carrying a bow) on the way to the forest where he will meditate before
celebrating the consecration of the 'Sacred Rite of Indra'.

■ NORTH GALLERY
In the first part of this gallery (**10**), only the lower part of the wall has reliefs and
some of them are unfinished. One panel is a circus—jugglers, acrobats and wrestlers.
The king presides over scenes of daily life. An animated procession of various animals
(pig, rhinoceros, rabbit, deer, puffer fish, lobster, and so on) is notable. (**At the other
end**), ascetics meditate in the forest and, on the banks of a river, a group of women
receive gifts. (**Near the door**), scenes of combat between the Khmers and the Chams.
The wall of the second part of the North Gallery (**11**) is almost entirely collapsed. (**At
each end**), the battle between the Khmers and Chams continues and the Khmers flee
to the mountain.

■ CORNER PAVILION (NORTHEAST)
Scenes of processions of Khmer warriors on elephants (**12**).

■ EAST GALLERY
The battle between the Khmers and the Chams continues (13). Towards the centre of this gallery the battle reaches a climax of action; elephants seem to be participating in the battle—one curls his trunk and tries to tear out the tusk of an opposing elephant. The Khmers appear finally to gain control of the battle.

■ THE INNER OR SECOND GALLERY
The galleries in this enclosure are separated by rooms, cells, and fragments—it is not a continuous aisle as on the exterior. Enter the interior gallery from the east, turn left, and continue moving in a clockwise direction with the reliefs on your right. The bas-reliefs depict, for the most part, mythological subjects of Hindu inspiration.

■ EAST GALLERY
(**Between two towers; right**) (1): Ascetics and animals in the forest and mountains. (**Small room; right**) (2): The king in his palace with ascetics. (**Above**): Rural and hunting scenes with lively animals; *apsarās* flying overhead. (**Facing and to the left**) (3): A military procession; this relief has the unusual feature of Khmer and Cham warriors intermixed; the lower tier comprises scenes of daily life.

■ CORNER PAVILION (SOUTHEAST)
Warriors march in procession led by a commander mounted on an elephant (4).

■ SOUTH GALLERY
Another military procession (5) and the warriors seem to be of the same nationality. Some genre scenes of everyday life: a man climbs a coconut tree, a Garuḍa and a giant fish at the base of Mount Meru with ascetics and animals. (The panel is very eroded and the scene is confused.)
 (**Small room**) (6): A fight between a ruler and an animal, possibly a lion, and (**left**) a hunter holds an elephant by the rear feet.
 (**The next two towers**) (7) (**On the wall; left**): a procession of warriors; (**facing, from left to right**), a scene of combat between a prince and his army; a palace and a cortège of musicians; (**lower tier**), a fisherman in a boat throws a net into the water while a princess watches; *apsarās* fly overhead.
 (**Between two towers**) (8): (**From the right**) (poor condition), (**facing**), a god standing on a lotus; (**from the left**), Śiva deformed and carrying the trident; (**above**), *apsarās* dance accompanied by an orchestra.
 (**Small room; from the right at the bottom**) (9): A genre scene of everyday life. (**Above**), Viṣṇu (four arms) descends towards Śiva (carrying a trident).
 In the last part of the South Gallery (10): A mountain with wild animals and a

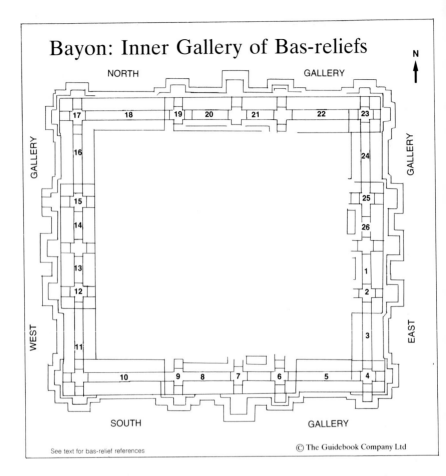

Bayon: Inner Gallery of Bas-reliefs

N

NORTH GALLERY

17 18 19 20 21 22 23

GALLERY

16

24

15

25

14

26

13

1

12

2

WEST

11

3

EAST

10 9 8 7 6 5 4

SOUTH GALLERY

See text for bas-relief references

© The Guidebook Company Ltd

tiger devouring a man; princesses walking amidst a group of *apsarās* dancing on lotuses. (**Above**), Śiva sitting in his celestial palace surrounded by his followers; ascetics and animals along the banks. A tiger pursues the ascetics while other devotees converse in the palace and several worshippers prostrate before the god. (**Centre**), Viṣṇu (four arms) is standing surrounded by flying *apsarās* and prostrating followers.

■ WEST GALLERY

Viṣṇu (four arms) is standing on a Garuḍa and subduing an army of demons (**11**).

(**Small room**) (**12**): A palace scene with *apsarās* dancing accompanied by an orchestra; (**above**), dancers and, above that, a battle scene.

(**Between two towers; right**) (**13**): Viṣṇu (four arms) superimposed on scenes of the construction of a temple—workers pulling a block of stone, polishing stone and hoisting blocks of stone into place. A nautical scene follows, with two people playing chess in a boat, and a cockfight. (**From left**), Śiva in a palace with Viṣṇu on his right; ascetics meditating in grottoes and swimming amongst lotus flowers; a bird holds a fish in its mouth.

(**Beyond the centre of the West Gallery**): A procession of warriors on horseback with two rulers sitting in chariots pulled by horses (**14**).

(**Small room**) (**15**): (**From the right**), a palace scene with people conversing and attendants dressing young princesses.

The most interesting relief in the next area (**16**) depicts the Churning of the Ocean of Milk; the body of the serpent with demons on the side of the head; the monkey Hanumān assists the gods on the side of the tail. A replica of the serpent crawls on the bottom of the ocean and is represented by a panel of fish; (**centre**), a column resting on the back of a turtle forms the pivot; Viṣṇu in his human form embraces the shaft. Other items are disks symbolizing the sun and the moon and a flask which is destined to contain the elixir of immortality. (**Left**), a god mounted on a bird seems to want to pacify a group of demons who are engaged in a battle; their chief stands in a cart drawn by superb lions.

■ CORNER PAVILION (NORTHWEST)
Another procession of warriors is depicted here (**17**).

■ NORTH GALLERY
Palace scenes (**18**); a procession of servants with offerings; a mountain inhabited by wild animals (elephants, rhinoceros, serpents). One boat carries men with short cropped hair and a chief with a trident and another one bears men wearing the head-dress of an inverted flower.

(**Small room**) (**19**) (**facing**): Śiva (ten arms) dances, with *apsarās* flying above. Viṣṇu (**right**) and Brahmā (four faces) (**left**), with Gaṇeśa; (**below**), Rāhu. (**Side of the wall**): Śiva sits between Viṣṇu and Brahmā; a charging boar.

(**Between two towers**) (**20**): (**right**), Śiva is surrounded by ascetics and women, with the bull Nandi nearby; (**facing**), ascetics meditating in the mountains. Kāma, the God of Love, shoots an arrow at Śiva, who is meditating at the top of a mountain with his wife Pārvatī at his side (for a description of this legend, see page 56–7).

(**Between two towers**) (**21**): (**From the right**), Śiva mounted on the bull Nandi with his wife Pārvatī sitting on his thigh. A palace, multiple-headed serpents and, (**below**), dancing *apsarās*.

An episode from the *Mahābhārata* follows, depicting 'Śiva grants a favour to Arjuna' (for a description of this legend see pages 57–8).

(**On the left of the door**): Another scene from the *Mahābhārata* of 'Rāvaṇa shakes

Mount Kailāsa' (for a description of this legend see page 57). Two scenes of the palace are superimposed on each other.

Servants with offerings (22); (above), ascetics meditating; Śiva blesses his worshippers, with flying *apsarās* above. A king leads a procession followed by his army (short-cropped hair), musicians, elephants and horses, princesses in palanquins and a cart pulled by oxen.

■ CORNER PAVILION (NORTHEAST)
Fragments of a procession (23).

■ EAST GALLERY
A military procession with musicians, foot soldiers

Head of a Cham warrior identified by a headdress that resembles an inverted lotus, after Delaporte

framed by horsemen and a chariot drawn by horses, a chariot (six wheels) mounted on sacred geese, the ark of the Sacred Fire, an empty throne and the king (carrying a bow) mounted on an elephant (24). (**After the door**), someone of rank (prostrating) at the feet of Śiva before going to battle.

(**Small room**) (25): Two large boats surrounded by fish in a pond. *Apsarās* and birds fly above.

(**Between two towers**) (26): The 'Legend of the Leper King'. (**From left to right**): The king fights against a serpent and a crowd watches. The serpent spews his venom on the king and he contracts leprosy. The king sits in his palace and gives orders to his servants who descend a staircase to consult with healing ascetics in the forest. Women surround the sick king and examine his hands. The king lies on the ground while an ascetic stands at his side.

Garuḍa holding a tail of a serpent in each hand; the capital, shaped like a lotus, reinforces the serpent theme and supports a figure of Hindu mythology

Chau Say Tevoda

Two symmetrical shrines, Thom Manon and Chau Say—alike in design and structure and twins also in ruin.[1]

Location: East of the Gate of Victory of Angkor Thom, across the road south from
Thommanon, 500 metres (1,640 feet) off the road
Access: Enter and leave Chau Say Tevoda by the north entrance
Date: End of the 11th century–first half of the 12th century
King: Sūryavarman II
Religion: Hindu
Art Style: Angkor Wat

BACKGROUND

Chau Say Tevoda and Thommanon are two small monuments close together (on the
left and right sides of the road) and similar in plan and style. Although the precise
dates of these monuments are unknown, they belong to the best period of 'classic' art
stylistically and represent two variations of a single theme of composition. Chau Say
Tevoda has deteriorated more than Thommanon.

LAYOUT

Chau Say Tevoda is rectangular in plan, with a Central Sanctuary opening to the east,
an enclosing wall with an entry tower in the middle of each side, and two libraries
opening to the west near the left and right sides of the enclosing wall at the east entrance.

Walking towards the temple one can see traces of a moat and vestiges of a laterite
base of an enclosing wall.

ENTRY TOWERS

The entry towers (1) are mostly demolished except for traces of the bases and stairways with sculpted steps. A raised causeway (3) on three rows of octagonal supports
(later than the monument) and a terrace link the east entry tower to a nearby river to
the east.

PEDIMENTS

At the south of the passage a scene depicts the combat of Sugrīva and Vali; at the
north of the passage (east side) the reliefs include monkeys, Śiva and Pārvatī on a
bull, and *apsarās*.

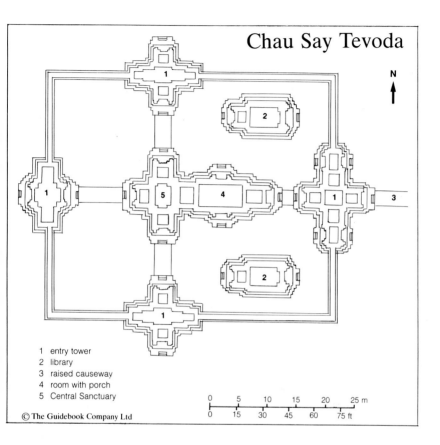

Chau Say Tevoda

N

1 entry tower
2 library
3 raised causeway
4 room with porch
5 Central Sanctuary

0   5   10   15   20   25 m
0   15   30   45   60   75 ft

© The Guidebook Company Ltd

CENTRAL SANCTUARY

A long room with a porch (4) precedes the square Central Sanctuary (5) connecting it with the east entry tower by a passage raised on three rows of columns of which only traces remain. This long room is covered with a pattern of flowers inscribed in squares and sculpted with stone flowers such as are seen at Banteay Srei and Bap-huon. The three false doors of the Central Sanctuary are decorated with foliage and columns with diamond-shaped patterns (lozenges) and flowers (on the left); human figures accentuate some of the bands of foliage in the columns.

[1]   R J Casey, *Four Faces of Śiva: The Detective Story of a Vanished Race*, p 181.

Kravan (Prasat): 'the cardamom sanctuary'

Location: East of Angkor Wat and south of Banteay Kdei
Access: Enter and depart from the east
Tip: The reliefs in this tower are best viewed in the morning when the east light enters the door; in the afternoon they are barely visible.
Date: The first half of the tenth century (921)
King: Completed during the reign of Harshavarman I (it may have been built by high court officials)
Religion: Hindu
Art Style: Transitional from Bakheng to Koh Ker

BACKGROUND

The main point of interest at Kravan is the sculpture on the interior of two of the five towers depicting Viṣṇu and his consort, Lakṣmī; the scene in the central tower is the most impressive one. These carvings in brick on the interior of a monument are unique in Khmer architecture.

This temple was reconstructed by the French and given a new foundation, interior walls and drains. Some broken bricks were replaced with carefully made reproductions which are marked with the letters 'CA', representing the Angkor Conservancy. These can be seen, for example, on both the interior and exterior of the tower on the right.

LAYOUT

Kravan is an unusual arrangement of five towers in a row on one terrace. They are built of brick; the lintels and columns are of sandstone.

CENTRAL TOWER

This is the only tower with recessed tiers intact which are visible on the interior. The columns are octagonal, with four bare sides and sandstone rings. This tower enclosed a *liṅga* on a pedestal. An inscription on the pillars gives the date 921 for the erection of the statue of Viṣṇu on the interior. **Decoration** (exterior): The east side of the Central Tower is sculpted with male guardians in shallow niches and chevrons and framed figures on the pilasters. A frieze of small heads adorns the lintel. **Decoration** (interior): The main decoration of this tower, on the **left**, depicts Viṣṇu taking three steps to span the universe and to assure the gods of the possession of the world. It comprises a standing image of Viṣṇu (with four arms) carrying his attributes—a disc, a ball, a conch and a club. One of his feet rests on a pedestal; nearby a person is meditating and another one is walking on a lotus held by a woman on a background of undulating lines representing the waves of the ocean. On the **right**, Viṣṇu on the shoulders of Garuḍa stands between two worshippers. **Facing**, Viṣṇu (with eight arms) is framed with six registers of people meditating and a giant lizard. This sculpture on brick was formerly coated with stucco and was probably highlighted with colours.

NORTH TOWER
This temple was dedicated to Lakṣmī, wife of Śiva. She holds the symbols of her powers in her four hands and is flanked by kneeling admirers; the niche with multiple lobes is decorated with tassels and floral swags.

SOUTH TOWER
The walls on the interior have no decoration. A lintel on the exterior with Viṣṇu on his mount, the Garuḍa, is skilfully modelled.

Krol Kō: 'the shed of the oxen'

Location: Northwest of Neak Pean, 100 metres from the road
Access: Enter and leave from the east
Date: Late 12th century–early 13th century
King: Jayavarman VII
Religion: Buddhist
Art Style: Bayon

BACKGROUND
The main items of interest at Krol Kō are the pediments on the ground. Two outstanding ones are a bodhisattva Avalokiteśvara standing on a lotus flanked by devotees and a strongly modelled scene of Kṛṣṇa lifting Mount Govardhana to shelter the shepherds.

LAYOUT
Krol Kō is a single tower monument with two enclosing walls built of laterite with an entry tower at the east and a moat with steps. There is a library built of laterite and sandstone opening to the west on the left of the interior courtyard. The Central Sanctuary stands on a terrace in the shape of a cross.

Mebon (East)

The lovely temple of Mebon, a pyramid of receding terraces on which are placed many detached edifices, the most effective being the five towers which crown the top. Could any conception be lovelier, a vast expanse of sky-tinted water as wetting for a perfectly ordered temple.[2]

Location: The East Mebon is 500 metres (1,640 feet) north of Pre Rup.
Access: Enter and leave the temple from the east entrance.
Date: The second half of the tenth century (952)
King: Rājendravarman II
Religion: Hindu (dedicated to Śiva); an ancestor temple in memory of the parents of the king
Art Style: Pre Rup

BACKGROUND

The Mebon stands on a small island in the middle of the Eastern Baray, which was a large body of water (2 by 7 kilometres, 1.2 by 4.3 miles) fed by the Siem Reap River. The temple was accessible only by boat. Today the *baray*, once a source of water for irrigation, is a plain of rice fields and the visitor is left to imagine the original majesty of this temple in the middle of a large lake.

LAYOUT

The East Mebon is a temple with five towers arranged like the numbers on a die atop a base with three tiers. The whole is surrounded by three enclosures. The towers represent the five peaks of the mythical Mount Meru.

The outer enclosing wall (1) is identified by a terraced landing built of laterite with two seated lions on each of the four sides (2). The interior of this wall is marked by a footpath. The next enclosing wall (3) is intercepted in the middle of each of its four sides by an entry tower in the shape of a cross (4). The towers are constructed of laterite and sandstone and have three doors with porches. An inscription was found to the right of the east tower. A series of galleries surrounds the interior of this enclosing wall (5). The walls are of laterite and have porches, sandstone pillars and rectangular windows with short balusters. The galleries were originally covered with wood and tiles but today only vestiges remain. They probably served as halls for meditation.

The stairways of the tiered base are flanked by lions (6). Beautiful monolithic elephants stand majestically at the corners of the first and second tiers (7). They are depicted naturalistically with fine detail such as harnessing. **Tip**: The elephant in the

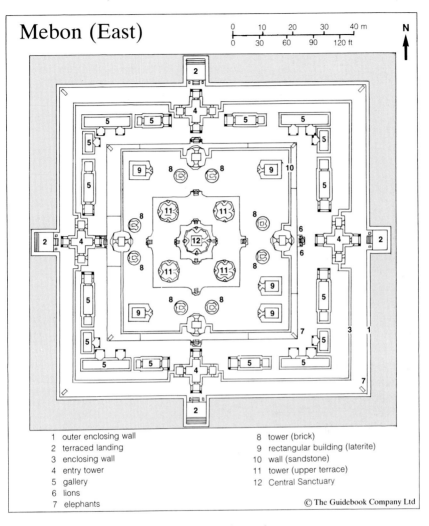

Mebon (East)

```
0    10    20    30    40 m
├────┼────┼────┼────┤
0     30    60    90   120 ft
```

N ↑

1	outer enclosing wall	8	tower (brick)
2	terraced landing	9	rectangular building (laterite)
3	enclosing wall	10	wall (sandstone)
4	entry tower	11	tower (upper terrace)
5	gallery	12	Central Sanctuary
6	lions		
7	elephants		© The Guidebook Company Ltd

best condition, and the most complete, is in the southwest corner.

ENTRY TOWERS
The lintels on the west entry tower (4) depict Viṣṇu in his *avatāras* of man-lion tearing the king of the demons with his claws (east). At the northeast corner Lakṣmī stands between two elephants with raised trunks sprinkling lustral water on her.

---

2   H Churchill Candee, *Angkor: The Magnificent, The Wonder City of Ancient Cambodia*, p 269.

INNER COURTYARD

The large inner courtyard contains eight small brick towers (**8**)—two on each side—opening to the east. Each one has octagonal columns and finely worked lintels with figures amongst leaf decorations. On the east side of the courtyard there are three rectangular laterite buildings (**9**) without windows opening to the west. The two on the left of the entrance are decorated with either scenes of the stories of the nine planets or the seven ascetics. Vestiges of bricks above the cornices suggest they were vaulted. There are two more buildings (without windows) of similar form at the northwest and southwest (**9**) corners of the courtyard.

UPPER TERRACE

The terrace with the five towers was enclosed by a sandstone wall with moulding and decorated bases (**10**). Lions guard the four stairways to the top platform.

CENTRAL SANCTUARIES

The five towers on the upper terrace were built of brick and open to the east; they have three false doors made of sandstone (**11** and **12**). Male figures on the corners are finely modelled. Circular holes pierced in the brick for the attachment of stucco are visible. The false doors of the towers have fine decoration with an overall background pattern of interlacing small figures on a plant motif.

LINTELS ON THE TOWERS OF THE UPPER LEVEL
■ CENTRAL TOWER

(**east side**): Indra on his mount, a three-headed elephant, with small horsemen on a branch; scrolls with mythical beasts spewing figures under a small frieze of worshippers; (**west side**): Skanda, God of War, rides his peacock; (**south side**): Śiva rides his sacred bull Nandi.

■ NORTHWEST CORNER TOWER

(**east side**): Ganeśa is curiously riding his trunk which is transformed into a mount.

■ SOUTHEAST CORNER TOWER

(**north side**): The head of a monster is eating an elephant.

Mebon (West)

Location: Four kilometres (2.4 miles) west of Angkor Thom
Access: The south dyke of the West Baray; take a boat to the island in the centre;
          walk to the east entrance of the temple.
Date: Second half of the 11th century
King: Udayadityavarman II
Religion: Hindu (probably dedicated to Viṣṇu)
Art Style: Baphuon

BACKGROUND
The West Mebon is situated at the centre of an artificial lake on a circular island with a diameter of about 150 metres (492 feet).

LAYOUT
The base for the temple was a square. A sandstone platform at the centre is linked to a causeway of laterite and sandstone that leads to the east dyke. The West Mebon was originally surrounded by a square enclosure with three square sandstone entry towers and a sanctuary on one level crowned with a lotus. Many towers have collapsed but the three on the east side are reasonably intact. The sides of the towers are carved with lively animals set in small squares, a type of decoration found only at the Baphuon. **Tip**: Walk along the shore line and look back at the island to see heaps of stones from the collapsed areas.

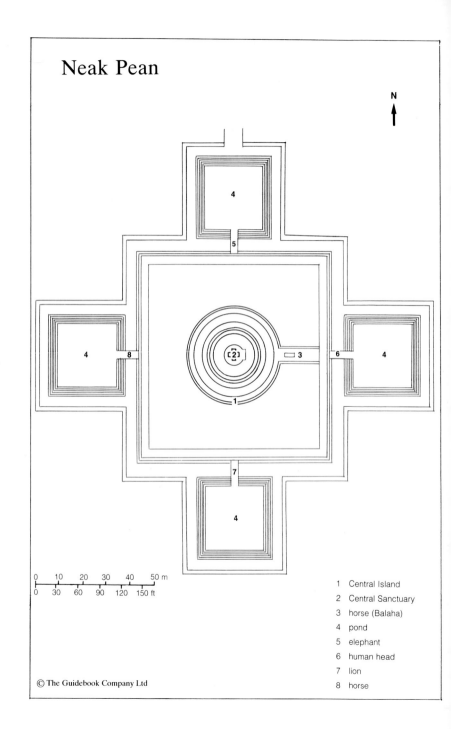

Neak Pean

N

0 10 20 30 40 50 m	
0 30 60 90 120 150 ft	

© The Guidebook Company Ltd

1 Central Island
2 Central Sanctuary
3 horse (Balaha)
4 pond
5 elephant
6 human head
7 lion
8 horse

Neak Pean: 'the coiled serpents'

Néak Pean is one of the temples that makes one dream of the olden days of luxury and beauty. It was worth while to live then and to be a woman among a race which has ever adored its women. It is to the overpowering temples of Civa that men and armies repaired; but it was at the tiny temple of Néak Pean that eager princesses laid their lovely offerings of wrought gold and pungent perfumes.[3]

Location: East of Prah Khan; 300 metres (984 feet) from the road
Access: Enter and leave from the north entrance
Date: Second half of the 12th century
King: Jayavarman VII
Religion: Buddhist
Art Style: Bayon

BACKGROUND

Although Neak Pean is small and a collection of five ponds, it is worth a visit for its unique features. It is believed to have been consecrated to Buddha coming to the glory of *nivāna*.

The central pond is a replica of Lake Anavatapta in the Himalayas, situated at the top of the universe. The lake gives birth to the four great rivers of the earth. These rivers are represented at Neak Pean by sculpted gargoyles corresponding to the four cardinal points. Lake Anavatapta was fed by hot springs and venerated in India for the curative powers of its waters. The orientation of the ponds at Neak Pean ensured that the water was always fresh because the ponds received only reflected light.

LAYOUT

Neak Pean is a large square man-made pond (70 metres, 230 feet each side) bordered by steps and surrounded by four smaller square ponds. A small circular island with a stepped base of seven laterite tiers is in the centre of the large square pond. Small elephants sculpted in the round originally stood on the four corners. The central tower was dedicated to Avalokiteśvara.

CENTRAL ISLAND (1)

The bodies of two serpents encircle the base of the island and their tails entwine on

---

Lotus Inspiration

...Néak Pean—the last word being pronounced 'Ponn', and the whole name signifies curved Nagas. Néak Pean is one of the temples that makes one dream of the olden days of luxury and beauty. It was worth while to live then and to be a woman among a race which has ever adored its women. It is to the overpowering temples of Civa that men and armies repaired; but it was at the tiny temple of Néak Pean that eager princesses laid their lovely offerings of wrought gold and pungent perfumes…Fancy it as it was in the old days. To begin with there was the artificial lake, a wide extent of water in the shallows of which floated the flowering lotus. In

Central Island at Neak Pean. This tree was destroyed by lightning in the 1950s

its exact centre—the surveyors of Angkor were expert—stood the exquisite miniature temple of one small chamber, the sanctuary, a temple as finely ornate and as well-proportioned as an alabaster vase. With art delicious this wonder was made to appear like a vision in the land of faerie. It floated upon a full-opened flower of the lotus, the petal tips curling back to touch the water. On the corolla of the flower, curved around the temple's base, were two Nagas whose tails were twisted together at the back and who raised their fan of heads on either side of the steps in front which mounted to the sanctuary. Thus they guarded the gem and gave gracious welcome to whosoever directed her light barque to draw close to this lovely heaven…On this circular pedestal of poetic imagination rested a square temple with four carved doors, one open occupying all the faśade except for the square columns which flank it. Above rose the tower with pointed over-door groups of carvings, symbolic, graceful, inspiring. Each closed door bore the figure of the humane god Vishnu standing at full height, but lest he impress too strongly his grandeur in this dainty spot, the space about him is filled with minor carvings which vary on each door.

Within this lovely casket was a seated stone figure. The door was ever open, suppliants might at any time lay before Buddha their offerings and their prayers.

The chamber was too small to admit them and they stood without in a bending group, swaying toward the Naga-heads for support or salaaming gracious salutations to the god of peaceful meditation. The golden boat floating beside the approach again…Rowers moved the shallop so slowly that the Naga-prow seemed to progress of its own volition. And so, the gods appeased, the spirits rose, and soft music spread over the waters in which the rich notes of male voices blended, and life went happily in the lovely twilight hour…one must know its former state to love it…Néak Pean stands hidden, but it stands in greater perfection than if it had not had the enveloping.

H Churchill Candee, Angkor: The Magnificent, The Wonder City of Ancient Cambodia (H F & G Witherby, London, 1925)

the west side. It is this configuration that gave the name of 'coiled serpents' to the temple. The heads of the serpents are separated to allow passage on the east. A blooming lotus surrounds the top of the platform, while lotus petals decorate the base.

CENTRAL SANCTUARY (2)

This is in the form of a cross, stands on two recessed levels, opens to the east and is crowned with a lotus. The three other doors are walled in and decorated with large images of Avalokiteśvara. The pediments depict episodes of the life of the Buddha: (**east**), 'the Cutting of the Hair'; (**north**), 'the Great Departure'; (**west**), 'Buddha Protected by a Serpent'.

The principal feature in the pond of the Central Sanctuary is a three-dimensional sculptured horse (3) swimming towards the sanctuary with figures clinging to its sides. The horse, Balaha, is a manifestation of the bodhisattva Avalokiteśvara, who has transformed himself into a horse to rescue Simhala, a merchant, and his companions of misfortune. They were shipwrecked on an island off Śrī Laṅkā and snatched by female ogres. The victims are holding on to the horse's tail in the hope of being carried ashore safely.

FOUR SMALL BUILDINGS

These buildings, one at the middle of each side of the central pond, are connected to it by an arched roof and open onto four small ponds with steps (4). The cavernous interior of the vault is decorated with panels of lotus and a waterspout in the form of an animal or human in the centre. The four buildings seem to have been for the ablutions of pilgrims. They anointed themselves with lustral water which flowed from the spout connected to the outside by a channel. Each water spout is different: (**north**), elephant head (5); (**east**), human head (6) (represents 'the Lord of Men' and is of very fine workmanship); (**south**), lion (7); (**west**), horse (8). The ceilings of these buildings are decorated with a lotus motif.

Zhou Daguan wrote that Neak Pean was:

> ... like a rich mirror, coloured by the stones, the gold and the garlands. This pool, of which the water is lit by the light of the golden prasat coloured by the red of the lotuses, shimmers in evoking the image of the sea of blood spilled by the Bhargara: on the interior there was an island taking its charm from the ponds which surround it, cleaning the mud of sin of those who came in contact with it, and serving as a boat to cross the ocean of existence.[4]

---

[4]   In M Glaize, *Les Monuments du Groupe d'Angkor*, p 212.

Palilay (Prah)

Location: North of Phimeanakas (see map page 80)
Access: Enter and leave the monument from the east.
Tip: The jungle around Prah Palilay is peaceful. Leave Tep Pranam and walk to Prah Palilay, then around the temple.
Date: Middle to last half of the 12th century
King: Jayavarman VII
Religion: Buddhist
Art Style: Angkor Wat

BACKGROUND
The presence of Buddhist monks and nuns at this temple give it a feeling of an active place of worship. Lintels and pediments lying on the ground at the sides and back of the temple afford a rare opportunity to see reliefs at eye level. Many depict Buddhist scenes with Hindu divinities.

LAYOUT
A large seated Buddha in front of the temple of Prah Palilay is of a recent date. A terrace in the shape of a cross precedes the temple and stands as an elegant example of the 'classic' period of Khmer art. Serpent balustrades terminating with a crest of seven heads frame the terrace. A causeway joins the terrace to the entry tower at the east set in the enclosing laterite wall, of which only parts remain. The entry tower is in the shape of a cross and has three passages and a cylindrical vault with a double pediment. The pediments of the entry towers are modelled with Buddhist scenes. The lintel on the east side of the entry tower depicts a reclining Buddha and the pediment on the south side has a finely carved seated Buddha; the pediment on the north has an uncommon depiction of a standing Buddha with his hand resting on an elephant. There are remains of two guardians (decapitated) on the east and two lions on the ground between the terrace and the Central Sanctuary.

CENTRAL SANCTUARY
Only the Central Sanctuary of Prah Palilay remains intact. The sandstone tower opens on four sides, each one of which has a porch. The tower stands on a base with three tiers and has a stairway on each side. On the upper portion there is a truncated pyramid that forms a sort of chimney, which is filled with reused stones.

Phimeanakas: 'aerial palace'

Location: Phimeanakas is located inside the enclosure of the Royal Palace of Angkor Thom north of Baphuon (see map page 80).

Access: Phimeanakas can be reached on foot either from Prah Palilay or from the Terrace of the Elephants. Pass through the gap in the south side of the enclosing wall of Prah Palilay and walk straight for about 200 metres (656 feet); turn left to the east and right at the first path, then follow it until you reach the temple. Or walk across the Terrace of Elephants at the entrance closest to the Victory Gate road and walk through an entry tower; then follow the path until you reach the temple. Alternatively, return to the main road beside the Terrace of the Leper King, turn right and turn right again on the first road, then drive straight to the monument. Enter Phimeanakas from the east entrance. It is possible to leave by the south gate and walk through a space in the enclosing wall to the east entrance of the Baphuon.

Tip: For those who want to climb to the Central Sanctuary, use the west stairway, which is in the best condition.

Date: Late tenth century–beginning of the 11th century

Kings: Jayavarman V and Udayadityavarman I

Religion: Hindu

Art Style: Kleang

BACKGROUND

The temple of Phimeanakas is situated near the centre of the area enclosed by the walls of the Royal Palace. It must originally have been crowned with a golden pinnacle, as Zhou Daguan described it as the 'Tower of Gold'. The temple is built of roughly hewn sandstone blocks and has little decoration.

According to legend there was a gold tower (Phimeanakas) inside the royal palace of Angkor the Great where a serpent-spirit with nine heads lived. The spirit appeared to the Khmer king disguised as a woman and the king had to sleep with her every night in the tower before he joined his wives and concubines in another part of the palace. If the king missed even one night it was believed he would die. In this way the royal lineage of the Khmers was perpetuated.

LAYOUT

The general plan of Phimeanakas is rectangular. The temple originally consisted of a Central Sanctuary on a tiered base and an enclosing wall. The grounds around the sanctuary included several courts and ponds.

A laterite wall encloses the temple and a second enclosing wall was built at a later date. Next there is a dry moat. The sandstone entry tower at the east is in the shape of a cross with two wings; the lintels have a central motif of a head of a *kāla* and the window frame is inscribed. These features are not shown on the plan. Leave the tower and walk towards the main sanctuary. On the right (north) there is a pond with moulding and laterite steps. It may have been a part of the palace reserved for women. Return to the centre walkway; after leaving the entry tower turn right and follow a path until you come to another large pond paved in laterite with sandstone steps. It was bordered by two stairways with bas-reliefs—along the side there are serpents in animal and human form surrounded by serpent-princesses; on the top there are male and female Garudas and mythical winged figures. This entire area was probably crowned by a serpent balustrade and may have served as a gallery for the sovereign and dignitaries of the court. It is separated from the north enclosing wall by paved causeways and from another pond on the east.

CENTRAL SANCTUARY (3)
The single sanctuary is on a base with three laterite tiers. It is approached by four steep stairways, one on each side (1). These stairways are framed by walls with six projections—two per step—decorated with lions. Elephants once stood on sandstone pedestals in the corners of the base but today they are mostly broken.

UPPER TERRACE
The upper terrace affords a spectacular view of the neighbouring temple of Baphuon. A narrow covered sandstone gallery (2) with windows and balusters at the edge of the upper terrace is a unique architectural feature. There were small pavilions at the corners but only vestiges remain.

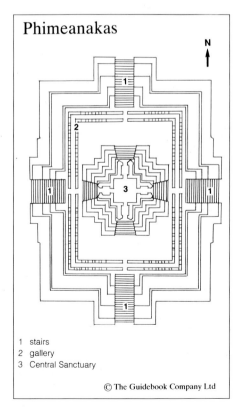

Phimeanakas

N

1 stairs
2 gallery
3 Central Sanctuary

© The Guidebook Company Ltd

Phnom Krom: 'the mountain below'

Location: Phnom Krom is approximately 12 kilometres (7.4 miles) southwest of Siem Reap near the north end of the Tonle Sap Lake. It is located on a mountain 137 metres (449 feet) high.

Access: Climb the steep stairs and curved path through a modern temple complex at the top of the hill. The walk affords a fine view of the lake and surrounding area.

Date: End of the ninth century–beginning of the tenth century

King: Yaśovarman I

Religion: Hindu (dedicated to the Hindu Trinity—Śiva, Viṣṇu and Brahmā)

Art Style: Bakheng

BACKGROUND

Yaśovarman I built a temple on each of the three hills dominating the plain of Angkor—Bakheng, Phnom Krom and Phnom Bok. The temple of Phnom Krom is visible from the aeroplane as one flies into Siem Reap.

LAYOUT

Phnom Krom is a square plan and consists of three towers in a row (1) situated dramatically on a hilltop. They were dedicated to Śiva, Viṣṇu and Brahmā respectively. The upper portions of the towers have collapsed and the façades are very degraded but otherwise they remain intact. The towers are enclosed by a laterite wall (2) intersected on each side by an entry tower in the shape of a cross (3). Three long halls built of laterite (only the bases of which remain) parallel the wall around the courtyard (4). They probably served as rest houses. Four small buildings inside the courtyard preceded the sanctuaries (5). They are similar except that the two at either end are brick and the two in the middle are sandstone. All four have a series of holes in the walls which suggests they may have been used as crematoriums.

CENTRAL TOWERS

The three central towers stand on a north–south axis on a low rectangular platform with moulding constructed of sandstone paving over a laterite base (6). Two sides of the base are intercepted by three stairways with lions on the landings. The towers are square and originally had four recessed tiers on the upper portion. They open to the east and west with false doors on the north and south. Traces of decoration remain around the base of the platform near the stairs, on the pilasters, the panels of the false doors, the cornices and on niches in the corners. The upper terrace affords a panoramic view of the Great Lake and the surrounding plain.

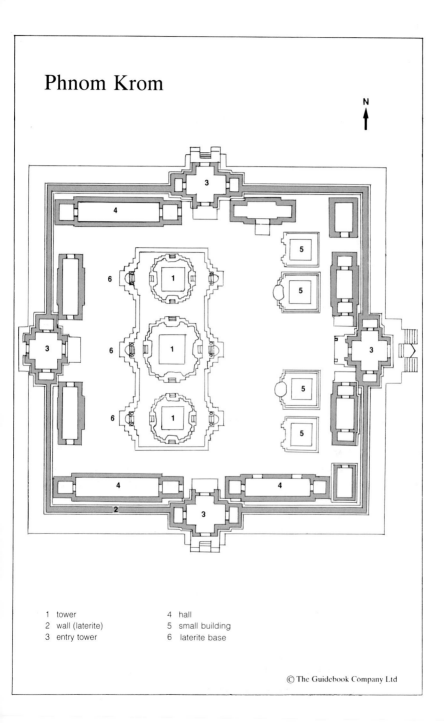

Phnom Krom

N
↑

1 tower
2 wall (laterite)
3 entry tower
4 hall
5 small building
6 laterite base

© The Guidebook Company Ltd

Prah Khan: 'the sacred sword'

Prah Khan, the Beguiler, the Romancer, and the artist...it is an entrancing mystery deep in the jungle, soft and alluring in the twilight made by heavy verdure, accessible only to the ardent lover of past days who is gifted with agility...They may have been courtyards where high priests gathered and guardians slept, but now they are walled bowers over which the trees extend to heaven's blue...It all seems a wondrous mass of beauty tossed together in superb confusion.[1]

Location: Prah Khan is north of Angkor Thom and west of Neak Pean.

Access: Enter and leave the temple from the west entrance (the description, however, begins at the east, the principal entrance). It is recommended you allow plenty of time for seeing this monument for 'there are delicious spots in which to stay still'. The World Monument Fund is in the process of clearing and repairing this temple to give visitors a better understanding of its original form.

Tip: When visiting Prah Khan follow the central artery on a west–east axis.

Date: Second half of the 12th century (1191)

King: Jayavarman VII

Religion: Buddhist (dedicated to the father of the king)

Art Style: Bayon

BACKGROUND

Four causeways lead to the temple and are bordered by the same figures (giants and gods) carrying a serpent as are found at the entrances to the city of Angkor Thom (not shown on the plan). This architectural element was the mark of a royal city. The absence of towers with faces such as those found at other temples built by the same king suggests Prah Khan is earlier. It may have served as a temporary residence of King Jayavarman VII while he was rebuilding the capital after the Chams sacked it in 1177.

Female divinity enclosed by a floral decorative element

Prah Khan shares similarities with the temple of Ta Prohm. The main elements are contained in a small space giving a cramped feeling. Much of the temple is in poor condition but even restored it would seem architecturally complex.

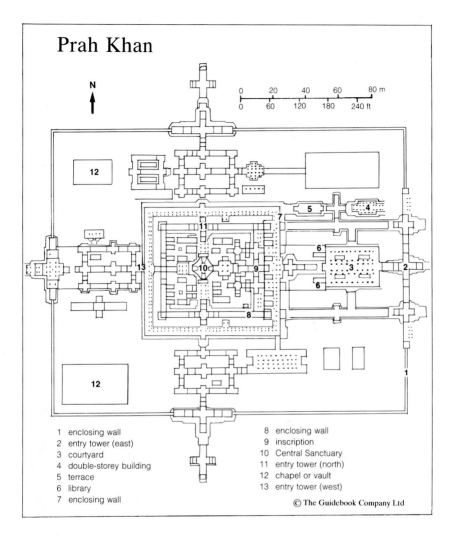

Prah Khan

N

| 0 | 20 | 40 | 60 | 80 m |
| 0 | 60 | 120 | 180 | 240 ft |

1 enclosing wall
2 entry tower (east)
3 courtyard
4 double-storey building
5 terrace
6 library
7 enclosing wall

8 enclosing wall
9 inscription
10 Central Sanctuary
11 entry tower (north)
12 chapel or vault
13 entry tower (west)

© The Guidebook Company Ltd

An inscription found in 1939 indicates Prah Khan was the ancient city of Nāgara-jayacri. The second part of the name, '-jayacri', is the Thai word for 'sacred sword', the meaning of Prah Khan. The sacred sword has a long history in Khmer tradition as in the late ninth century Jayavarman II left his successor a sacred sword, the Prah Khan, which descendants still guard. Cœdès, though, suggests that the legend of the sacred sword may have originated with the Thais who still call their sacred sword 'Jayacri'.

[1]   H Churchill Candee, *Angkor: The Magnificent, The Wonder City of Ancient Cambodia*, pp 274–81.

LAYOUT

Prah Khan comprises a vast area of 140 acres (56.7 hectares) and four enclosing walls. The buildings are enclosed by a rectangular wall 700 by 800 metres (2,296 by 2,624 feet) and surrounded by a moat (not shown on the plan). Inside is a labyrinth of pavilions, halls and chapels.

A processional way with stone markers displaying the head of a mythical monster and a niche, which originally contained a seated Buddha, precedes a causeway bordered by gods and demons holding a serpent, which leads to an outer enclosing wall.

Giant Garuḍas and serpents are seen in relief on the laterite wall, a motif that is reproduced every 50 metres (164 feet) around the three-kilometre (1.9-mile)-long wall. The entry tower at the east has three porches and the centre one forms a passage to the temple (not shown on the plan). The walls are decorated with a tapestry pattern with a base of scrolls, small female divinities and false windows with lowered blinds.

On the right of the avenue leading to the enclosing wall are the remains of a rest house for pilgrims, as described in the inscription of the temple (not shown on the plan). They have thick walls and windows with a double row of balusters.

THE SECOND ENCLOSURE

The second enclosure (1) is preceded by a large terrace with two levels; lions and serpent balustrades lead to an imposing entry tower with five doors and two end pavilions (2). It connects to galleries with columns on the exterior and a wall with false windows and balusters on the interior (toward the courtyard).

Inside the second enclosure marked by a laterite wall is a courtyard in the shape of a cross (3) with four smaller courtyards surrounded by galleries with columns. Traces of vaults are visible and above the bays are friezes of *apsarās* This area is known as the Hall of Dancers.

On the right there is a series of large thick pillars set close together on two levels. The function of this double-storey building (4) is unknown, although some archaeologists suggest it may have been a library and no trace of a stairway between the two floors has been found. Others believe it housed the sacred sword after which the temple was named. On the opposite side there is a long terrace (5) raised on laterite retaining walls.

Base of a pillar decorated with geometric bands, lotus petals and rosettes, illustrated in Voyage au Cambodge, *Delaporte, 1880*

> *It is the night of a feast—the birthday of a king or the holiday of a god. Fires are burning in Pra Khan and in Ta Prohm and Bantei Kedei. There is a ruddy glow in the sky above Angkor Thom, and the pyramid of the eastern Mebon is an inverted flame in the still water of the baray. And the close-packed millions of the people of Angkor are on the roads with torches in their hands. Patterns of light weave across the blackness of the plain. Streams of fire are flowing in weird channels, welding at the unseen cross-roads and spreading out in dazzling tapestries in the temple courts.*
>
> *R J Casey,* Four Faces of Śiva: The Detective Story of a Vanished Race
> *(George G Harrap, London, 1929)*

Return to the central artery and continue walking across the dancing hall and into a courtyard. On the left and right there are libraries (**6**) opening to the west. The next gallery is finely decorated with female and male divinities in high relief framing the bays and a frieze of Buddha images separated by flying figures with Garuḍas in the corner.

Through two enclosing walls (**7** and **8**), there is a stone stele in a portico to a central shrine (**9**). It is inscribed on each of the four faces.

CENTRAL SANCTUARY
The Central Sanctuary (**10**) divides the courtyard into two unequal sections. The main tower with four porches is in the shape of a cross. The centre of the interior is marked by dome-shaped stone mound that tapers to a point (sixteenth century). This is a good vantage point from which to see the perspective of rooms and galleries in the cardinal directions and the interplay of light and shade.

A stroll to the south of the Central Sanctuary, from where one can see the surrounding jungle, is most pleasant. A walk to the north, from where a causeway bordered by gods and demons is visible, is equally rewarding. The entry tower on the north side (**11**) is framed by trees. The main porch of this entrance is preceded by large guardian figures and a terrace in the shape of a cross.

Return to the Central Sanctuary and continue to the west. The structures on the left and right (**12**) in the courtyard were probably funerary chapels or family vaults. The entry tower of the enclosure at the west is in the shape of a cross with pillars and aisles (**13**).

Pre Rup: 'turn, or change, the body'

'A work of great dignity and impeccable proportions', wrote Maurice Glaize
of Pre Rup in his guidebook of 1963.

Location: Northeast of Srah Srang and 500 metres (1,640 feet) south of the south end
of the East Baray

Access: Enter and leave the monument from the east entrance. To climb to the
upper terrace use the east stairway; it is slightly less steep than the others.

Tip: Because the temple is built entirely of brick and laterite, the warm tones of
these materials are best seen early in the morning or when the sun is setting. There are two views from the top terrace: the first looking east
towards Phnom Bok and the mountain chain of Phnom Kulen; and the
second looking west where the towers of Angkor Wat can be distinguished
on the far horizon.

Date: Second half of the tenth century (961)

King: Rājendravarman II

Religion: Hindu (dedicated to the god Śiva)

Art Style: Pre Rup

BACKGROUND

The boldness of the architectural design of Pre Rup is superb and gives the temple
fine balance, scale and proportion. The temple is almost identical in style to the East
Mebon, although it was built several years later. It is the last real 'temple-mountain'.
Pre Rup was called the 'City of the East' by Philippe Stern, a Frenchman who worked
on the site.

The Cambodians have always regarded this temple as having funerary associ-
ations but the reason is unknown. The name Pre Rup recalls one of the rituals of
cremation in which the silhouette of the body of the deceased, outlined with its ashes,
is successively represented according to different orientations. Some archaeologists
believe that the large vat located at the base of the east stairway to the central area was
used at cremations.

LAYOUT

Pre Rup dominates the vast plain which the East Baray irrigated. Constructed on an
artificial mountain in laterite with brick towers, the plan is square and comprises two
enclosures (**1** and **2**) with four entry towers each and a base with three narrow tiers
(**3**) serving as a pedestal for five towers on the top platform—one in each corner and
one central (**4**). The outer enclosing wall is 127 by 116 metres (417 by 380 feet).

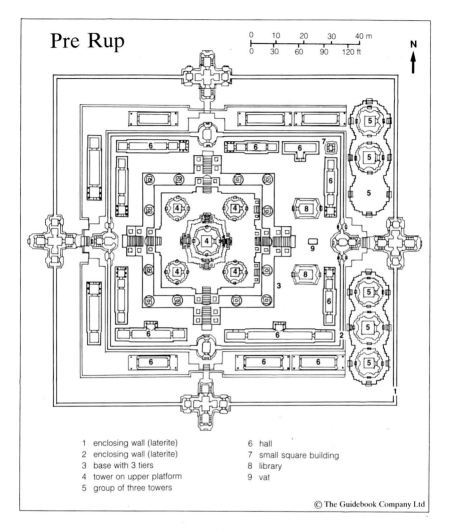

Pre Rup

0 10 20 30 40 m
0 30 60 90 120 ft

N

1 enclosing wall (laterite)
2 enclosing wall (laterite)
3 base with 3 tiers
4 tower on upper platform
5 group of three towers

6 hall
7 small square building
8 library
9 vat

Inside the outer laterite enclosing wall there are two groups of three towers, one on each side of the entrance (5); the towers of each group share a common base. The middle tower in each of the two groups dominates and is more developed than the others. It appears that the first tower on the right was never built or, if it was, its bricks were reused somewhere else. The most complete lintel is on the tower at the far left (south) on the east face showing Viṣṇu in his *avatāras* as a man-lion.

The next enclosure, also made of laterite, has four small entry towers, one on each side (2). Long galleries surround the courtyard on the interior. The walls of these galleries, which have sandstone porches, are built of laterite.

In the courtyard there are vestiges of long rest halls (6) probably used by pilgrims. They have sandstone pillars in the east and laterite walls and windows with balusters in the west. In the northeast corner there is a curious small square building (7) built of large blocks of laterite and open on all four sides. The inscription of the temple was found in a gallery near this building.

LIBRARIES

On the left and right sides of the east entry tower of the second enclosure there are libraries (8) with high towers. They sheltered carved stones with motifs of the nine planets and the seven ascetics. In the centre there is a vat (9) between two rows of sandstone pillars. Glaize suggested that this might have been, rather than a sarcophagus, a base for a wooden building or for a statue of Nandi, the sacred bull, the mount of Śiva to whom the temple was dedicated.

CENTRAL AREA (BASE AND TOWERS) (3, 4)

The square base has a stairway on each side. Pedestals flanking the stairways are adorned with seated lions of which those on the lower terraces are larger than those on the higher levels. The first two tiers are built of laterite and have simple supporting walls with a moulded base and cornice. The third tier is built of sandstone. Two supplementary stairways are framed with lions on the east side. Twelve small temples opening to the east and containing *linga* are evenly spaced around the first tier. The upper platform is raised on a double base of moulded sandstone with stairways flanked with lions.

The five central towers on the top platform are open to the east. They all have three false doors made of sandstone and are sculpted with figures and plant motifs. Traces of plaster are visible on the tower in the southwest corner. At the same tower there is a depiction of Sarasvatī, wife of Brahmā, with four faces and arms. On the west side of this tower there is another divinity with four arms and heads in the form of a wild boar; it is the wife of Viṣṇu in his *avatāras* as a boar. Figures in the niches are surrounded by flying *apsarās* at the corners of the towers. The figures at the two west towers are feminine while those at the east and central towers are masculine.

The Roluos Group of Monuments

Three temples—Bakong, Lolei and Prah Kō—11 kilometres (6.8 miles) southeast of the Siem Reap Market, comprise the Roluos group of monuments (see map below). They are close together and extend over an area of three kilometres (1.9 miles) east of the Great Lake. The Roluos group, dating from the late ninth century, is the earliest site of the 600-year Angkor Period that is open to visitors. The three temples belonging to this important group have similar characteristics of architecture, decoration, materials and construction methods, which combine to reveal the beginning of the 'Classic Period' of Khmer art.

BACKGROUND

Roluos is the site of an ancient centre of Khmer civilization known as Hariharālaya ('the abode of Hari-Hara'). Some 70 years after Jayavarman II established his capital on Mount Kulen in 802 inaugurating the Angkor Period, the king moved the capital to Hariharālaya, perhaps for a better source of food or for defence purposes. He died at Roluos in 850. It is generally believed that his successors remained there until the capital was moved to Bakheng in 905.

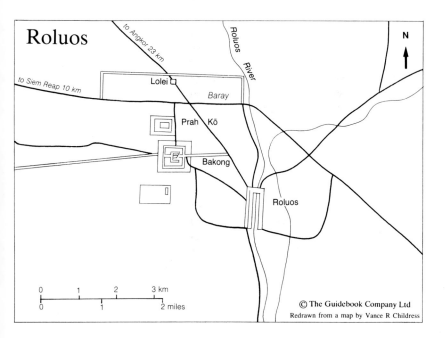

Roluos

to Angkor 23 km

to Siem Reap 10 km

Roluos River

Lolei

Baray

Prah Kō

Bakong

Roluos

N

0   1   2   3 km
0   1   2 miles

© The Guidebook Company Ltd
Redrawn from a map by Vance R Childress

(following pages) *Three towers at Prah Kō dedicated to ancestors*

ARCHITECTURE

The buildings of the Roluos group are distinguished by tall square-shaped brick towers on pedestals. They open to the east, with false doors on the other three sides. As is typical of this period, brick was used for the towers and sandstone for carved areas such as columns, lintels and decorative niches.

A wall originally enclosed the temples though only traces remain today. It was intersected on two or more sides by an entry tower, an innovation of this period, or perhaps slightly earlier. The early examples were square with a tiered upper portion.

The library also made its appearance at Roluos. It is a rectangular building with a curved roof and pediments. A temple often has two libraries, one on each side of the entry tower preceding the Central Sanctuary.

DECORATION

The characteristic decorative features of the Roluos group are: a *kāla* (monster head), the Hindu god Viṣṇu on his mount the Garuḍa, female figures with abundant jewellery, and a preponderance of guardians and *apsarās*.

Columns are generally octagonal and intricately adorned with delicate leaves. Decoration on the lintels at Roluos is, according to some art historians, 'the most beautiful of all Khmer art'.

Bakong

Location: Bakong is located at Roluos south of Prah Kō.
Access: Enter and leave the temple at the east. A modern Buddhist temple is
            situated to the right of the east entrance to Bakong.
Date: Late ninth century (881)
King: Indravarman I
Religion: Hindu (dedicated to Śiva)
Art Style: Prah Kō

BACKGROUND

Bakong was the centre of the town of Hariharālaya, a name derived from the god Hari-
Hara, a synthesis of Śiva and Viṣṇu. It is a temple-mountain representing the cosmic
Mount Meru. Four levels leading to the Central Sanctuary correspond to the worlds
of mythical beings (*nāgas*, Garuḍas, *rākṣasas* and *yakṣas*).

LAYOUT

The temple of Bakong is built on an artificial mountain and enclosed in a rectangular
area by two walls. It has a square base with five tiers. The first, or outside, enclosure
(not on the plan) (900 by 700 metres, 2,953 by 2,297 feet) surrounds a moat with an
embankment and causeways on four sides which are bordered by low *nāga* balustrades. The second and smaller enclosure (1) has an entry tower (2) of sandstone and
laterite in the centre of each side of the wall. There were originally 22 towers inside
the first enclosures. After passing through the entry tower at the east one comes to a
long causeway (3) decorated with large seven-headed serpents across a moat. Long
halls (4) on each side lie parallel to the eastern wall. They were probably rest houses
for visitors. Two square-shaped brick buildings at the northeast and southeast (5)
corners are identified by rows of circular holes and an opening to the west. The vents
in the chimneys suggest these buildings served as crematoriums. There was originally
a single building of this type at the northwest and southwest corners but today they
are completely ruined. On each side of the causeway just beyond the halls there are
two square structures with four doors (6). The inscription of the temple was found in
the one on the right.

   Further along the causeway, there are two long sandstone buildings (7) on each
side which open to the causeway. These may have been storehouses or libraries. To
the north and south of the storehouses respectively there is a square brick sanctuary
tower (8). There are two more on each side of the central platform, making a total of
eight. Decoration on the towers is in brick with a heavy coating of stucco. The towers, with one door opening to the east and three false doors, have a stairway on each

Roluos: Bakong

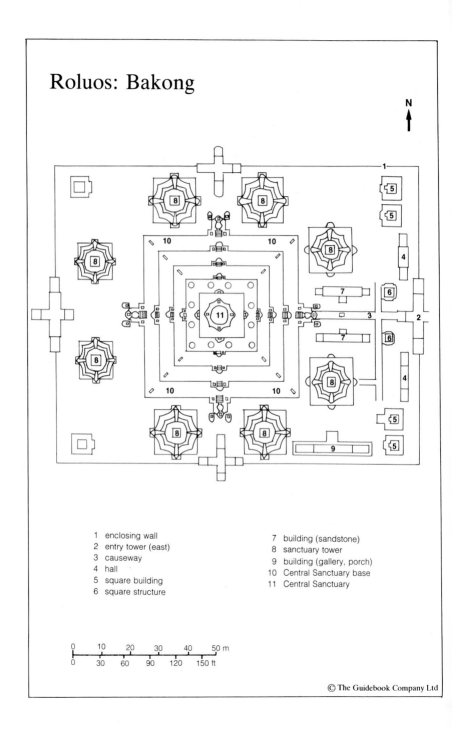

N

1 enclosing wall
2 entry tower (east)
3 causeway
4 hall
5 square building
6 square structure

7 building (sandstone)
8 sanctuary tower
9 building (gallery, porch)
10 Central Sanctuary base
11 Central Sanctuary

0   10   20   30   40   50 m
0   30   60   90   120   150 ft

© The Guidebook Company Ltd

side which is decorated with crouching lions at the base. The two to the east of the central platform have a unique feature, a double sandstone base. The door entrances and the false doors were uniformly cut from a single block of sandstone. The decoration on the false doors is exceptionally fine, especially that on the tower on the right in the front row, the false door of which has remarkable *kāla* handles. The corners of the towers are decorated with female and male guardians in niches. **Tip**: The lintels of the west towers are in the best condition.

A long building with a gallery and a porch opening to the north (9) is situated close to the western wall (on the left); it is mostly demolished.

CENTRAL AREA (BASE AND TOWERS)

The square-shaped base (10) has five tiers with a stairway on each of the four sides and, at the base, a step in the shape of a moonstone. Remains of a small structure can be seen at the base of the stairway flanked by two sandstone blocks which may have held sculpted figures.

Elephants successively smaller in size stand at the corners of the first three tiers of the base. The fourth tier is identified by twelve small sandstone towers, each of which originally contained a *linga*. The fifth tier is framed by a moulding decorated with a frieze of figures (barely visible). The ones on the south side are in the best condition.

CENTRAL SANCTUARY

The Central Sanctuary (11) is visible from each of the five levels because of the unusual width of the tiers. The sanctuary is square with four tiers and a lotus-shaped top. Only the base of the original Central Sanctuary remains. The rest was constructed at a later date, perhaps during the twelfth century.

Lolei

Location: Lolei is at Roluos, north of Bakong. A modern Buddhist temple is located in the grounds of Lolei near the central towers.
Access: Enter and leave the temple by the stairs at the east.
Tip: Beware of the ants during certain seasons near the top of the entrance steps.
Date: End of the ninth century (893)
King: Yaśovarman I
Religion: Hindu (dedicated to Śiva); in memory of the king's father
Art Style: Transitional between Prah Kō and Bakheng

BACKGROUND

Although Lolei is small it is worth a visit for its carvings and inscriptions. The temple of Lolei originally formed an island in the middle of a *baray* (3,800 by 800 metres, 12,467 by 2,625 feet), now dry. According to an inscription found at the temple the water in this pond was for use at the capital of Hariharālaya and for irrigating the plains in the area.

LAYOUT

The layout consists of two tiers with laterite enclosing walls and a stairway to the upper level in the centre of each side. Lions on the landings of the stairways guard the temple. A sandstone channel in the shape of a cross situated in the centre of the four towers on the upper terrace is an unusual feature. The channels extend in the cardinal directions from a square pedestal for a *linga*. It is speculated that holy water poured over the *linga* flowed in the channels.

CENTRAL SANCTUARIES

Four brick towers with tiered upper portions, arranged in two rows, on the upper terrace make up the Central Sanctuaries. As the two north towers are aligned on the east–west axis, it is possible the original plan had six towers which probably shared a common base like that at Prah Kō. **Tip:** The northeast tower is the best preserved.

The entrances of the doors to the towers are cut from a single block of stone, as at Bakong. The corners of the towers on the east are decorated with male guardians holding tridents and those of the west with female divinities holding fly whisks. They are sculpted in sandstone with a brick casing. The panels of the false doors have multiple figures. The inscriptions on the door frames are exceptionally fine.

The workmanship on the lintels is skilled and the composition balanced. Some noteworthy depictions are: Indra on an elephant with figures and *makaras* spewing serpents (northeast tower); Viṣṇu riding a Garuḍa with a branch of serpents (southeast tower).

Prah Kō: 'the sacred ox'

Location: Prah Kō is located at Roluos between Bakong and Lolei; it is mid-way between Bakong and the road.
Access: Enter and leave the temple from the east
Date: Late ninth century (879)
King: Indravarman I
Religion: Hindu (dedicated to Śiva); funerary temple built for the king's parents, maternal grandparents, and a previous king, Jayavarman II and his wife
Art Style: Prah Kō

LAYOUT

The complex of Prah Kō is square and surrounded by four enclosing walls with entry towers successively smaller in size. The first two walls are in a ruined state with only vestiges remaining. The first, or outer, enclosure is 450 by 800 metres (1,476 by 2,625 feet) square with entry towers on the east and west sides.

The central area is rectangular and consists of six brick towers arranged in two rows on a low platform. The towers to the front of the platform are larger than those at the back; the middle one in the front is the largest and set slightly back from the other two. The three in the front row are for paternal ancestors, with male guardians flanking the doorways; the three in the back row are for maternal ancestors and have female divinities flanking the doorways. The back row of towers is curiously un-evenly spaced with the right-hand one closer to the centre tower than the left-hand one. It has been suggested that the placement of the two towers close together in the back may signify that those two ancestors loved each other during their earthly life.

A small terrace in the shape of a cross (largely destroyed) (1) precedes the laterite entry tower to the east (2). Additional wings on the east and west sides lead to a lat-erite causeway. Sandstone pillars and windows with thick balusters carved with rings, which give the appearance of being turned like wood, complete the remains of the temple complex. A step at the entrance in the shape of a moonstone is note-worthy for its graceful form.

In the courtyard there are the bases of two galleries which run parallel to the east wall (3). Close to and parallel to the north and south walls of the enclosure are two long halls (4). On each side of the causeway, and closer to it, are two galleries with a porch opening to the east (mostly ruined) (5). Between the long hall and the gallery on the left is a square brick building (6) that may have been a crematorium, with a tiered upper portion and a porch opening to the west. It is distinguished by rows of holes (perhaps for ventilation) and a row of figures of ascetics in niches above the holes on the upper portion of the building.

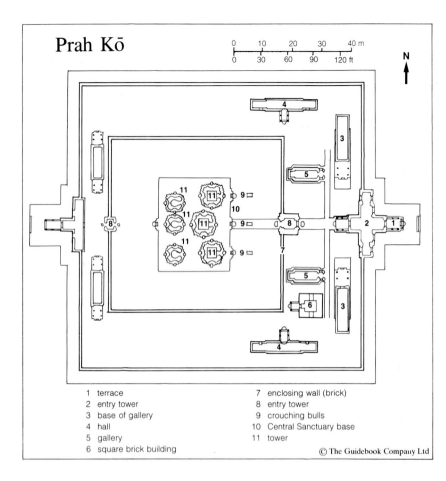

Prah Kō

0 10 20 30 40 m

0 30 60 90 120 ft

N

1 terrace	7 enclosing wall (brick)
2 entry tower	8 entry tower
3 base of gallery	9 crouching bulls
4 hall	10 Central Sanctuary base
5 gallery	11 tower
6 square brick building	© The Guidebook Company Ltd

Continuing along the causeway one comes to the brick wall of an enclosure (7) which has two entry towers, one on the east and another directly opposite it on the west (8). They are simple square buildings with columns and fine lintels depicting Viṣṇu on a Garuḍa. An inscription was found in the entry tower on the east. Past the entry tower at the east in the courtyard there are the remains of three crouching sacred bulls aligned in a row (9).

CENTRAL AREA (BASE AND TOWERS)
The base of the Central Sanctuaries has three stairways along the eastern side (10). The landings are decorated with male and female figures. Sandstone lions on the stairways guard the temple. The only other access to the central level is a single stairway on the west side.

The central towers are square on the lower portion with a porch in each of the cardinal directions (11). Each of the six towers of the Central Sanctuary group was covered with stucco. Traces of the original material can be seen on the tower on the right of the back row. The thickness of the stucco and the sandstone motifs of the false doors are features on this tower. The columns, which are octagonal, are 'incontestably the most beautiful of Khmer art', according to French conservators. The frame of the door is cut in four parts and the corners where the pieces meet are mitred, like wood, by cutting the ends of two pieces at identical angles and fixing the cut faces together.

Sandstone lintels above the doors of the tower in the front row on the right are decorated with small horsemen and figures mounted on serpents. The lintels on the false doors of the middle tower of the back row have a Garuda in the centre, surmounted by a row of small heads.

Corner niches of the central tower in the front row have male guardians in niches carved in sandstone and encased in brick.

The decoration on the three towers in the back row is of inferior quality to that on those in the front row. The corner niches contain female deities. A curious feature of the centre tower in the back row is that the false door is brick coated with stucco whereas the other false doors are of sandstone.

Each tower originally contained an image of a Hindu god with whom the deceased was united.

Tip: Looking east from the platform of the Central Sanctuaries one can see the laterite roadway and remains of the entry towers of the four enclosing walls.

Leaving the Central Sanctuary from the west one passes through a simple square entry tower with a stairway (mostly demolished). The courtyard on this side is narrow and contains two rectangular galleries parallel to the west wall.

Spean Thma: 'the bridge of stone'

Location: 200 metres (656 feet) east of Thommanon
Access: Walk to the side of the road and down the path

BACKGROUND
Spean Thma is a bridge constructed of reused blocks of sandstone of varying shapes and sizes which suggests it was built to replace an earlier one. The orientation of the bridge seems odd today because the course of the river has changed. The river now flows along the right side of the bridge instead of under its arches.

LAYOUT
The bridge is supported on massive pillars, the openings between them spanned by narrow corbel arches. There are reportedly traces of 14 arches. See map page 76.

Srah Srang: 'the royal bath'

It was perhaps a chapel to Kama, God of Love. The spot would suit the temper of the strange power, terribly strong and yet terribly tender, of that passion which carries away kingdoms, empires, whole worlds, and inhabits also the humblest dwellings...Love could occupy this quiet nest embedded in water...gave the impression that love had come one day and had left there, when he went away, a part of his spirit.[1]

Location: Across the road from the east entrance of Banteay Kdei
Access: Enter and leave Srah Srang from the road
Tip: Srah Srang always has water and is surrounded by greenery. According to one French archaeologist, it 'offers at the last rays of the day one of the most beautiful points to view the Park of Angkor'.
Date: End of the 12th century
King: Jayavarman VII
Religion: Buddhist
Art Style: Bayon

BACKGROUND
Srah Srang is a large lake (700 by 300 metres, 2,297 by 984 feet) with an elegant landing terrace of superb proportion and scale.

LAYOUT

A majestic platform ('landing stage') with stairs leads to the pond. It is built of laterite with sandstone moulding. The platform is in the shape of a cross with serpent balustrades flanked by two lions. At the front there is an enormous Garuda riding a three-headed serpent. At the back there is a mythical creature comprising a three-headed serpent, the lower portion of a Garuda and a stylized tail decorated with small serpent heads. The body of the serpent rests on a dais supported by mythical monsters. See map page 76.

Suor Prat (Prasat):
'the towers of the cord dancers'

Location: At the beginning of the road leading to the Gate of Victory of Angkor
Thom; 1,200 metres (3,937 feet) in front of Phimeanakas
Access: Enter and leave the towers from the road at the east
Date: End of the 12th century
King: Jayavarman VII
Religion: Buddhist
Art Style: Bayon

BACKGROUND

The purpose of these towers is a source of some controversy. According to a Cambodian legend, the towers served as anchoring places for ropes which stretched from one to another for acrobats performing at festivals, while the king observed the performances from one of the terraces. This activity is reflected in the name of the towers. Zhou Daguan wrote about an entirely different purpose of the towers in describing a method of settling disputes between men.

> *Twelve little stone towers stand in front of the royal palace. Each of the contestants is forced to be seated in one of the towers, with his relatives standing guard over him. They remain imprisoned two, three, or four days. When allowed to emerge, one of them will be found to be suffering some illness—ulcers, or catarrh, or malignant fever. The other man will be in*

---

[1]   P J de Beerski, *Angkor: Ruins in Cambodia*, pp 189–90.

perfect health. Thus is right or wrong determined by what is called 'celestial judgement'.[2]

Henri Mouhot wrote that the towers were 'said to have been the royal treasure...It served, they say, as a depository for the crown jewels'.[3] Another theory is that they may have served as an altar for each province on the occasion of the taking of the oath of loyalty to the king.

LAYOUT
Prasat Suor Prat is a row of 12 square laterite and sandstone towers, six on either side of the road leading to Angkor Thom, parallel to the front of the terraces. The two towers closest to the road are set back slightly from the others. The towers are connected by galleries and are of similar style and construction. The towers have an unusual feature of windows with balusters on three sides. Entrance porches open toward the square and the road to the Gate of Victory of the city of Angkor Thom. These features support the theory that these towers were used as some sort of viewing area, reserved for princes or dignitaries, opening on to the large square of the Royal Palace. The interior of each tower has two levels and on the upper one there is a cylindrical vault with two pediments. The frames, bays and lintels were made of sandstone. See map page 80.

Ta Keo: 'the ancestor Keo or the tower of crystal or glass'

The majestic ziggurat of Ta Keo, most enigmatic of the minor fanes, stepping up toward the sun with a dignity and power suggestive of Angkor Vat. It is dripping with green and crowned with trees, but is still supreme over the forest. Its rocky masses, rising above the tops of the coconut palms, convey the impression that it only recently emerged from some cavern underground, carrying the forest with it in its rocketing ascent. Ta Keo's lack of ornament makes it distinctive among the works of the Khmers, who were so prodigal of decoration. But its very simplicity gives it architectural importance. Its plan shows the development of a new spirit in the people, the growth of good taste.[4]

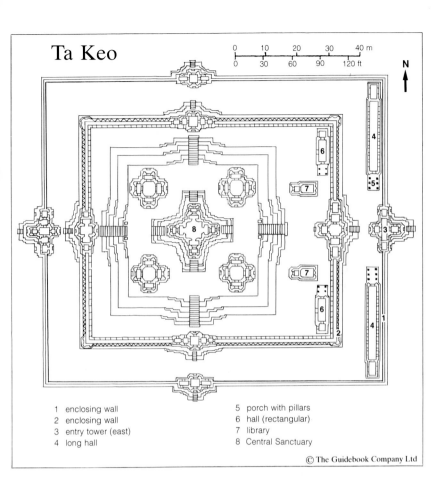

Ta Keo

Scale:
0 10 20 30 40 m
0 30 60 90 120 ft

N

1 enclosing wall
2 enclosing wall
3 entry tower (east)
4 long hall

5 porch with pillars
6 hall (rectangular)
7 library
8 Central Sanctuary

© The Guidebook Company Ltd

Location: East of Thommanon and Chau Say Tevoda

Access: Enter and leave by the south or east entrances

Tip: The ascent to this temple is steep and because of its orientation a visit in the morning is preferable.

Date: End of the tenth century to early 11th century

King: Jayavarman V to Sūryavarman I

Religion: Hindu (dedicated to Śiva)

Art Style: Kleang

---

2   Chou Ta-Kuan (Zhou Daguan), *The Customs of Cambodia*, p 33.

3   Henri Mouhot, *Travels in the Central Parts of Indo-China (Siam), Cambodia, and Laos*, p 8.

4   R J Casey, *Four Faces of Śiva: The Detective Story of a Vanished Race*, p 181.

BACKGROUND

An unusual aspect of this temple is that it remains unfinished, the reason for its non-completion is unknown. Had it been finished, Ta Keo would undoubtedly have been one of the finest temples at Angkor. It is an imposing sight, scaling 22 metres (72 feet) to the sky, and gives an impression of power. Ta Keo is the first temple built entirely in sandstone and as such serves as a milestone in Khmer history. Enormous blocks of stone were cut to a regular size and placed in position. The absence of decoration at Ta Keo gives it a simplicity of design that separates it from the other monuments.

LAYOUT

Ta Keo is square in plan with five towers arranged like the dots on the face of a die and stands majestically on a terrace that is 12 metres (39 feet) high with three tiers. It is a representation of Mount Meru. The base has fine moulding. The temple has two enclosures (1 and 2) with entry towers on each side. There are inscriptions on the pilasters of the east entry tower (3). The first two tiers of the platform form the base of two courtyards. One is enclosed by a wall and the other by a gallery; the gallery is too narrow to permit walking around.

The east entrance to Ta Keo is marked by a causeway over a moat that is preceded by lions and boundary stones (not shown on the plan). The entry tower in the exterior wall was made of sandstone with a central tower and three passages. On each side of the east wall there was a long hall (4) that was probably a shelter for pilgrims. It was preceded by a porch with pillars (5).

The second terrace has a moulded laterite base with four sandstone entry towers, one on each side. It is surrounded by a sandstone gallery lit by windows on the interior. The gallery completely surrounds the terrace and has openings on each of the four sides. On the east there are two long halls (6) of the same type as the rest halls on the first terrace. Two libraries (7) open to the west.

CENTRAL AREA

The upper level is square and stands on a tiered base with stairways on each side. Most of the space on the upper level is occupied by the five towers, all unfinished, opening to the four cardinal points. The Central Sanctuary (8) dominates the layout. It is raised above the other towers and is given further importance by the development of porches and pediments. The interior of the central tower is undecorated.

Line drawing of decoration on a lintel with a register of floral swags

Decoration around the base of a pyramid with a diamond-shaped geometrical motif and floral centres

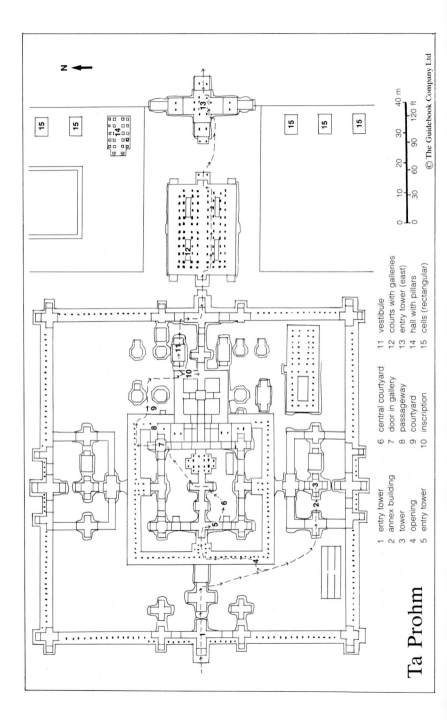

Ta Prohm

N

1 entry tower
2 annex building
3 tower
4 opening
5 entry tower

6 central courtyard
7 door in gallery
8 passageway
9 courtyard
10 inscription

11 vestibule
12 courts with galleries
13 entry tower (east)
14 hall with pillars
15 cells (rectangular)

0   10   20   30   40 m
0 30 60 90 120 ft

© The Guidebook Company Ltd

Ta Prohm: 'the ancestor Brahmā'

Ta Prohm's state of ruin is a state of beauty which is investigated with delight and left with regret.[5]

Location: Ta Prohm is located southwest of the East Mebon and east of Angkor Thom. Its outer enclosure is near the corner of Banteay Kdei.
Access: Enter the monument from the west and leave from the east entrance.
Tip: Ta Prohm is especially serene and beautiful in the early morning. A torch and a compass are useful for visiting this temple at all times.
Date: Mid-12th century to early 13th century (1186)
King: Jayavarman VII
Religion: Buddhist (dedicated to the mother of the king)
Art Style: Bayon

BACKGROUND

Ta Prohm is the 'undisputed capital of the Kingdom of the Trees'. It has been left untouched by archaeologists except for the clearing of a path for visitors and structural strengthening to stave off further deterioration. Because of its natural state, it is possible to experience at this temple the wonder of the early explorers when they came upon these monuments in the middle of the nineteenth century.

Shrouded in dense jungle the temple of Ta Prohm is ethereal in aspect and conjures up a romantic aura. Fig, banyan and kapok trees spread their gigantic roots over stones, probing walls and terraces apart, as their branches and leaves intertwine to form a roof over the structures. Trunks of trees twist amongst stone pillars. 'The strange, haunted charm of the place entwines itself about you as you go, as inescapably as the roots have wound themselves about the walls and towers', wrote a visitor 40 years ago.

A Sanskrit inscription on stone, still in place, gives details of the temple. Ta Prohm owned 3,140 villages. It took 79,365 people to maintain the temple including 18 great priests, 2,740 officials, 2,202 assistants and 615 dancers. Among the property belonging to the temple was a set of golden dishes weighing more than 500 kilograms, 35 diamonds, 40,620 pearls, 4,540 precious stones, 876 veils from China, 512 silk beds and 523 parasols.[6] Even considering that these numbers were probably exaggerated to glorify the king, Ta Prohm must have been an important and impressive monument.

---

[5]   H Churchill Candee, *Angkor: The Magnificent, The Wonder City of Ancient Cambodia*, p 256.
[6]   G Cœdès, *Angkor: An Introduction* (Oxford University Press, Singapore, 2nd ed, 1990), p 96.

LAYOUT

Ta Prohm is among the largest of the monuments in the Angkor complex. The inscription gives an idea of the size of the temple. The complex included 260 statues of gods, 39 towers with pinnacles and 566 groups of residences.[7] Ta Prohm comprises a series of long low buildings standing on one level, which are enclosed by a rectangular laterite wall (600 by 1,000 metres, 1,959 by 3,281 feet). Only traces of the wall are still visible. The centre of the monument is reached by a series of towers connected with passages. This arrangement forms a 'sort of sacred way into the heart of the monument'. Three square galleries enclose the area.

Tip: Some areas of the temple are impassable and others are accessible only by narrow dark passages. It is recommended to follow the plan with a route and landmarks indicated or to stay with a guide to avoid getting lost.

The boundaries of the exterior wall are recognizable on the west by a stone entry tower in the shape of a cross, with an upper portion in the form of four faces, one looking towards each of the cardinal points (not shown on the plan). The approach to the west entrance of the temple is a path through the forest. After about 350 metres (1,148 feet) there is a stone terrace in the shape of a cross. Remains of lions, serpent balustrades and mythical creatures lie scattered in the area. Walk across the terrace to the vestibule of the enclosing wall. The view from this point is spectacular.

> *Everywhere around you, you see Nature in this dual role of destroyer and consoler; strangling on the one hand, and healing on the other; no sooner splitting the carved stones asunder than she dresses their wounds with cool, velvety mosses, and binds them with her most delicate tendrils; a conflict of moods so contradictory and feminine as to prove once more—if proof were needed—how well 'Dame' Nature merits her feminine title!*[8]

The next causeway with serpent balustrades on each side leads to an entry tower (1) in the first enclosure around the temple. Inside, on the right, niches along the inner wall contain images of the Buddha. Return to the centre of the vestibule, turn right and walk through the courtyard to the annex building at the right (2). Continue walking straight through the series of rooms and passages to a tower (3). The relief on the horizontal beam is a fine representation of a scene from 'The Great Departure': when the future Buddha decides to leave his father's palace to live the life of a monk, the gods hold the hoofs of his horse so those sleeping in the palace are not awakened.

Return to the courtyard and pass through an opening (4) in the wall of the second enclosure (at the south end). The roots of a tree grip the double row of pillars in this gallery. Walk to the centre of the complex, turn right and enter the entry tower

(5) of the third enclosing gallery. The inner walls are decorated with friezes of pendants, scrolls and figures in niches. Turn right again and walk into the central courtyard (6) of the temple.

CENTRAL SANCTUARY
Follow the plan and walk through the Central Sanctuary, recognizable by its undecorated interior. The stone has been hammered, presumably to apply a coating, probably of paint or gilt. Evenly spaced holes in the wall from floor to ceiling suggest a covering of wood, stucco or metal.

Walk across the central courtyard towards the left (northeast) and through the door (7) of a gallery that is framed by the roots of a tree. Turn left and walk through a dark passageway (8) and a courtyard (9). Enter the aisle with pillars, turn right, walk straight between twin towers and to the right into a very narrow passage which houses the inscription (10) of the temple. Return by the same passage, turn right and continue straight, passing through a vestibule (11). The false doors on the north and south sides of the large rectangular enclosure with high walls are finely decorated. There are four small courts with galleries and pillars (12). Ritual dances may have been performed in this area.

Walk across the courtyard and into the entry tower of the enclosing wall, at the east entrance (13). It is in the shape of a cross with pillars on the interior, four wings and two passages on the side. The walls of these passages are decorated with reliefs. To the left there is a hall with pillars placed close together (14). They probably provided the base for a structure built of wood. Beyond are small rectangular cells (15) which surround the exterior of Ta Prohm.

One leaves Ta Prohm by a path (400 metres, 1,312 feet long) leading to the exterior enclosure where sections of the wall are visible.

> *So the temple is held in a stranglehold of trees. Stone and wood clasp each other in grim hostility; yet all is silent and still, without any visible movement to indicate their struggle—as if they were wrestlers suddenly petrified, struck motionless in the middle of a fight. The rounds in this battle were not measured by minutes, but by centuries.*[9]

[7]   M Glaize, *Les Monuments du Groupe d'Angkor*, p 184.

[8]   H W Ponder, *Cambodian Glory: The Mystery of the Deserted Khmer Cities and their Vanished Splendour*, p 305.

[9]   Rt Hon M MacDonald, *Angkor and the Khmers*, 4th ed, 1965, p 115.

Ta Som: 'the ancestor Som'

Location: East of Neak Pean
Access:　Enter and leave by the east entrance
Date:　　End of the 12th century
King:　　Jayavarman VII
Religion: Buddhist (dedicated to the father of the king)
Art Style:Bayon

BACKGROUND
Ta Som has not been restored. It is a small quiet temple and affords a delightful visit. In the past one of the significant features of Ta Som was the growth of fig trees in the

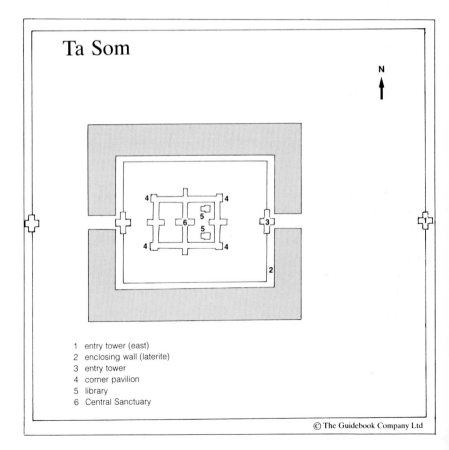

Ta Som

1　entry tower (east)
2　enclosing wall (laterite)
3　entry tower
4　corner pavilion
5　library
6　Central Sanctuary

© The Guidebook Company Ltd

faces at the entrance towers. These have been cut from the east tower but they are still visible at the west one.

LAYOUT

Ta Som is a single tower monument on one level surrounded by three enclosing walls with entry towers on the east and west carved with four faces. The face on the right of the east tower (1) (facing the temple) has a beautiful smile. The entry towers are in the shape of a cross with a small room on each side connecting to a laterite wall.

Walk through the first entry tower over a causeway which crosses a moat and is bordered with serpents and large Garuḍas. The wall of the second enclosure is in laterite (2) with a sandstone entry tower in the shape of a cross on the east and west sides (3). The entry towers have windows with balusters on the exterior and are preceded by a porch with pillars.

The next enclosure comprises a laterite and sandstone gallery with corner pavilions (4) which have moulded false doors. Amongst the crumbled heaps of stones in the courtyard are two libraries (5) opening to the west.

CENTRAL SANCTUARY

The main tower (6) is in the shape of a cross with four porches. To see the Central Sanctuary, courtyard and libraries, climb through the opening on the north side.

Tep Pranam: 'the worshipping god'

Location: 100 metres (328 feet) north of the Terrace of the Leper King
Access: A long path from the road leads to Tep Pranam.
Tip: This is one of the most serene areas in the park of Angkor. A visit to this area should not be rushed and should also include Prah Palilay.
Date: end of the ninth century
King: Yaśovarman I
Religion: Buddhist

LAYOUT

The entrance to Tep Pranam is marked by a laterite causeway bordered by double boundary stones at the corners and a terrace in the shape of a cross. The sandstone walls of the base of the temple have a moulded edging. Two lions precede the walls and there are serpent balustrades which are of a later date. See map page 80.

BUDDHA

The large Buddha seated on a lotus pedestal is on a moulded base and coated in sandstone. The body of the Buddha has been reassembled from numerous stones.

Terrace of the Elephants

An Imperial hunt in the sombre forests of the realm. There are formidable elephants...The forest in which they travel is impenetrable to all but tiny creatures, able to squeeze their smallness between the fissures of the undergrowth, and to the biggest animals, which crush chasms for their passage in the virgin vegetation. The elephants are ridden by servants and princes, and tread as quietly as if they were on an excursive promenade. Their steps of even length have no respect for any obstacle.[10]

Location: In the Royal Square of Angkor Thom
Access: From the road at the east
Date: End of the 12th century
King: Jayavarman VII
Religion: Buddhist
Art Style: Bayon

BACKGROUND

The terrace faces on to the Royal Square of the city of Angkor Thom. This area was the Royal Palace but the actual buildings were built of wood and have not survived.

The Terrace of the Elephants shows evidence of having been rebuilt and added to; and it is believed that alterations took place during the reign of Jayavarman VII at the end of the twelfth or the beginning of the thirteenth century. It is situated in front of the east entry tower of the enclosing wall at the Royal Palace.

LAYOUT

The Terrace of the Elephants (see map page 80) is over 300 metres (984 feet) long and extends from Baphuon to the Terrace of the Leper King. It has three platforms. The south stairway is framed with three-headed elephants gathering lotus flowers with their trunks, which form columns. The walls of the platforms are decorated with lions and Garudas which support the central stairway. Several projections above are marked by lions and there are serpent balustrades with Garudas on the dais.

The main part of the façade of the terrace is decorated with elephants depicted in profile. 'All the pachyderms, almost life-size, are magnificent...and the whole effect has an indescribable splendour.'[11] They depict realistic hunting scenes with elephants killing with their trunks and tigers clawing the elephants. They are surmounted by a balustrade of serpents on the dais.

The top of the terrace has two levels: one is square and another is a platform, on

The façade of the Terrace of the Elephants, Angkor Thom

the base of which are moulded sacred geese. It is believed that this area originally contained wooden pavilions highlighted with gold.

HORSE WITH FIVE HEADS

A large sculpted horse stands at the base of an inner wall located at the stairway before the forked path off the main road with a tree stump in the middle. On this platform and to the right, towards the Terrace of the Leper King, there is an inner wall with a sculpted panel, which must have been part of an ancient façade. It depicts a horse with five heads and is an exceptional piece of sculpture, lively and remarkably worked. It is the horse of a king, as indicated by the tiered umbrellas over his head; the horse is surrounded by *apsarās* and menacing demons armed with sticks pursuing several people who bear a terrified expression. Some French savants believe this is a representation of Avalokiteśvara in the form of the divine horse Balaha (see the description of the temple of Neak Pean, page 164, for details of this horse). Recent clearing at the Terrace of the Elephants has revealed another five-headed horse of the same size and proportion to the left of the first one.

---

[10]   P J de Beerski, *Angkor: Ruins in Cambodia*, p 147.
[11]   P J de Beerski, *Angkor: Ruins in Cambodia*, p 148.

Terrace of the Leper King

The stone monarch is absolutely naked, his hair is plaited and he sits in the Javanese fashion. The legs are too short for the torso, and the forms, much too rounded, lack the strong protuberances of manly muscles; but, however glaring are his defects, he has many beauties, and as a study of character he is perhaps the masterpiece of Khmer sculpture. Whilst his body is at rest his soul boils within him...His features are full of passion, with thick lips, energetic chin, full cheeks, aquiline nose and clear brow...his mouth, slightly open, showing the teeth. This peculiarity of the teeth being shown in a smile is absolutely and strangely unique in Cambodian art.[12]

Location: Immediately to the north of the Terrace of the Elephants
Access: From the road
Tip: Be sure to ask the guide to show you the inner wall
Date: End of the 12th century
King: Jayavarman VII
Religion: Buddhist
Art Style:Bayon

BACKGROUND

The outer wall of the terrace bears bas-reliefs (see below). During clearing the French found a second wall with bas-reliefs similar in composition to those of the outer wall. Some archaeologists believe that this second wall is evidence of a change in plan by the architects. Others have suggested that it symbolizes the part of the cosmic mountain Meru under the ground which is allegedly equal in size to the part above ground.

LEPER KING

The statue of the Leper King on the terrace is a copy. The original is in the courtyard of the National Museum in Phnom Penh. The Leper King is seated with his right knee raised. Some art historians consider this posture to be 'Javanese style'. Unusual features of this statue are that he is naked and has no indication of sexual organs. The iconography of the so-called 'Leper King' is uncertain. Some historians think the figure represents Kubera, god of wealth, who allegedly was a leper. There is an inscription on the statue in characters of the fourteenth or fifteenth century which may be translated as the equivalent of 'the Assessor of Yama', god of death or of judgement. Cœdès believes that most of the Khmer monuments were funerary temples and that the remains of kings were deposited there after cremation. He thinks, therefore, that the royal crematorium was located on the Terrace of the Leper King. The statue, then, represents the god of death and is properly situated on the terrace to serve this purpose.

A legend in a Cambodian chronicle tells of a minister who refused to prostrate before the king, who hit him with his sword. Venomous spittle fell on the king who then became a leper and was called the Leper King. And although some historians believe that Jayavarman VII was a leper and for that reason built many hospitals throughout the empire, there is no historical evidence to support the theory that the king was a leper.

LAYOUT
The Terrace of the Leper King is supported by a base 25 metres (92 feet) long. The sides are faced in sandstone and decorated with bas-reliefs which are divided into seven registers. See map page 80.

BAS-RELIEFS (EXTERIOR WALL)
Mythical beings—serpents, Garudas and giants with multiple arms, carriers of swords and clubs, women with a naked torso and a triangular coiffure with small flaming discs—adorn the walls of the terrace. **Tip**: The north side of the exterior wall is the best preserved. Return to the south side and enter the interior corridor.

BAS-RELIEFS (INTERIOR WALL)
These reliefs are in remarkable condition. Walk along the corridor and enjoy a close-up view of the deeply carved scenes arranged in registers. The themes are similar to those on the exterior and include a low frieze of fish, elephants and the vertical representation of a river.

---

[12] P J de Beerski, *Angkor: Ruins in Cambodia*, p 175.

Thommanon

Location: East of the Gate of Victory of Angkor Thom, across the road (north) from Chau Say Tevoda, 500 metres (1,640 feet) from the road
Access: Enter and leave Thommanon by the south entrance
Date: End of the 11th century–first half of the 12th century
King: Sūryavarman II
Religion: Hindu
Art Style: Angkor Wat

BACKGROUND

Thommanon is a gem and should not be missed. It is similar in plan and style to Chau Say Tevoda, which is close by. For details on the background, see Chau Say Tevoda, page 152.

LAYOUT

Thommanon is rectangular in plan with a sanctuary (1) opening to the east, a moat and an enclosing wall with two entry towers, one on the east and another on the west (2), and one library (3) near the southeast side of the wall. Only traces of a laterite base of the wall remain.

CENTRAL SANCTUARY

The base of the tower is finely modelled and decorated; the foliage of the middle band has raised figures. There are four porches, one on each side of the central tower. The decoration on the three false doors of these porches is exceptionally delicate. Also notice the highly stylized, yet exquisite, female divinities. The east lintel depicts Viṣṇu on a Garuḍa.

A porch with tiers on the east entry tower connects with a long hall (4) which has a false attic. The pediment above the south door is in poor condition, but the scene is recognizable: it is Rāvaṇa (with multiple heads and arms) trying to shake the mountain where Śiva is enthroned. On the interior, above the door toward the joining vestibule, the death of Vali after his battle against Sugrīva is depicted.

ENTRY TOWER (EAST)

This is linked at the base to the long hall. The entrance has three passages and bays that have been walled in. The centre has five porches, the one to the west being a double porch (5). Cylindrical vaulting can be seen on one recessed level. The pediment on the north depicts Viṣṇu felling two of his enemies, one of whom he holds by the hair.

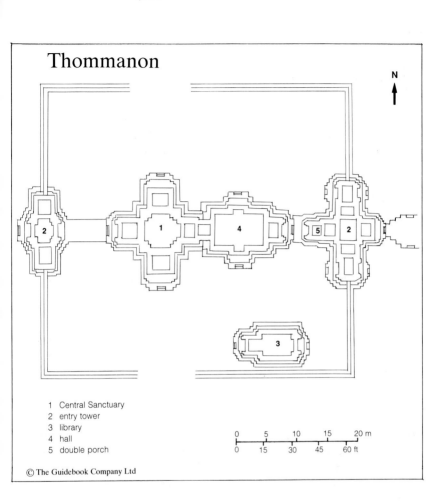

Thommanon

N

1 Central Sanctuary
2 entry tower
3 library
4 hall
5 double porch

0   5   10   15   20 m
0   15   30   45   60 ft

© The Guidebook Company Ltd

LIBRARY

The library has a false attic with elongated windows with balusters that have been walled in. The centre is paved with laterite; it opens to the west with a small porch and two windows; there is a false door on the east side.

ENTRY TOWER (WEST)

This entry tower has a central passage and two wings with windows. The building shows absolute purity of lines in its architecture and great care has been taken with the decoration. The west pediment depicts Viṣṇu on a Garuḍa battling against the demons. The columns and the base are ornamented with human figures; the false tiles on the end of the vaults represent lions.

The West Baray

The West Baray is a vast man-made lake (2 by 8 kilometres, 1.24 by 4.96 miles) in replica of and slightly larger than the East Baray (see map page 76). It is surrounded by a levy of earth which forms a dyke. According to legend, the young daughter of a ruler of Angkor was grabbed by an enormous crocodile which made a large opening in the south dyke of the West Baray that can still be seen today. The crocodile was captured and killed. The princess, still living in its stomach, was rescued.

Tip: The view from the southwest corner of the *baray* is splendid, especially at sunset.

As the temple in the middle is in the same style as the Baphuon, the *baray* was probably constructed in the eleventh century. The east dyke leads to the temple of Bakheng. Some historians believe the West Baray could have been a mooring place for the royal barges as well as a reservoir and a site for breeding fish. It was used as a landing field for seaplanes in the middle of this century and during the reign of Prince Sihanouk his foreign visitors water-skied on this lake.

Additional Sites

CHAPEL OF THE HOSPITAL

Location: East of Thommanon, Chau Say Tevoda and Spean Thma; on the right of the road just past the Siem Reap River

Access: Enter and leave the monument from the east

Date: End of the 12th century

King: Jayavarman VII

Religion: Buddhist

Art Style: Bayon

BACKGROUND
An inscription found in the area gives details of the hospitals built by Jayavarman VII and confirms the identity of this site as one of the 102 hospitals built by the king.

LAYOUT
Traces of an entry tower of sandstone and laterite in the shape of a cross at the east remain. A short causeway precedes the single tower of this site.

The Central Sanctuary is in the shape of a cross opening to the east and with false doors on the other three sides. Female divinities adorn the exterior and a scroll surrounds the base of the tower. The pediments are decorated with images of the Buddha.

THE KLEANGS: 'STOREHOUSE'

Location: The Kleangs are located behind the twelve towers of Prasat Suor Prat and facing the Terraces of the Elephants and the Leper King.

Access: Enter and leave from the west; walk past the Suor Prat towers towards the east.

Date: End of the 10th century–beginning of the 11th century

King: Jayavarman V or Sūryavarman I

Religion: Hindu

Art Style: Kleang

BACKGROUND

The North and South Kleangs consist of a pair of large sandstone façades that look quite grand against a jungle background. They are similar in time, layout, style and decoration, although inscriptions suggest that the South Kleang was built slightly later than the North one. Some scholars believe the name 'storehouse' is inappropriate for these buildings and suggest they may have been reception halls for receiving foreign dignitaries.

LAYOUT

Both buildings are long rectangular structures with a porch in the shape of a cross in the middle of the west and east sides. Windows with balusters are evenly spaced across the front on each side of the porches. The decoration is restrained but thoughtful in its design and execution. The faceted columns of the doorways support lintels decorated with foliate scrolls.

North Kleang: The workmanship of the architecture and decoration is more carefully executed than at the South Kleang. At the back of the North Kleang a laterite wall with horizontal windows at the top encloses smaller halls in a courtyard.

South Kleang: The long rectangular building is unfinished but it stands on a base with moulding. In the interior decoration is limited to a frieze under the cornice.

PRASAT BEI

Location: Between the southern moat of Angkor Thom and Baksei Chamkrong; 175 metres (574 feet) west of Thma Bay Kaek

Access: Enter and leave the monument from the east

Date: Tenth century
Religion: Hindu (dedicated to Śiva)

LAYOUT

Prasat Bei is a group of three towers that share a common base and open to the east. The towers are built of brick and the walls of the base are of laterite. The tower on the left (north) is unfinished. Both the left and right towers are missing their tops and thus look truncated. A lintel on the tower in the centre depicts Indra on his mount, an elephant with three heads. A liṅga on a pedestal is in the interior of this tower.

TA PROHM KEL

Location: On the left of the road going from the west entrance to Angkor Wat to the south gate of Angkor Thom
Access: Enter and leave the monument from the east
Date: End of the 12th century
King: Jayavarman VII
Religion: Buddhist
Art Style: Bayon

BACKGROUND

Ta Prohm Kel is a single tower that was one of the 102 hospitals built by Jayavarman VII. According to Cœdès, the monument is associated with the legend of Pona Krek. A beggar who was paralyzed was cured at this site by the god Indra. The legend is supported by the discovery of stones depicting the bodhisattva Avalokiteśvara, the healer.

LAYOUT

Ta Prohm Kel consists of a single tower with only the main level intact. It stood on a moulded and decorated base, opened to the east and had three false doors. Female divinities adorn the corners of the tower and scrolls surround the base.

THMA BAY KAEK:
'THE ROCK THAT IS A PLACE TO PUT RICE FOR THE CROWS'

Location: Between the southern moat of Angkor Thom and Baksei Chamkrong; 125 metres (400 feet) west of the road
Access: Along a path; the monument is on the right
Date: Tenth century
Religion: Hindu (dedicated to Śiva)

BACKGROUND
Little remains of this temple, but it is worth seeing for its setting and can be combined with a visit to Prasat Bei. An undisturbed deposit of gold leaves was found under the Central Sanctuary.

LAYOUT
Thma Bay Kaek consists of a single tower built of bricks on a square plan. Only the base remains and the sandstone frame of a door with a lintel. A terrace with laterite steps preceded the tower.

Espying the Ethereal City of Nakhon Wat

'I had already been in Siam several months before I could carry out the project which had originally taken me to that country. My plan was to cross overland into Cambodia, and there photograph the ruined temples and examine the antiquities which have been left behind by the monarchs of a once powerful empire. Mr. H. G. Kennedy, of H.B.M.'s consular service, consented to accompany me on this expedition, and we got away together on January 27, 1866.

. . . The Chow Muang of Nakhon Siamrap received us with great courtesy, placing a house at our disposal for two or three days, until a Laos chief, who had come with a considerable escort on a pilgrimage to Nakhon Wat, should have started on his homeward journey, and left room for our accommodation. The old town of Siamrap is in a very ruinous state—the result, as was explained to us, of the last invasion of Cambodia—but the high stone walls which encircle it are still in excellent condition. Outside these fortifications a clear stream flows downwards into the great lake some fifteen miles away, and this stream, during the rainy season, contains a navigable channel. On the third morning of our stay we mounted our ponies, and passed out of the city gates on the road for Nakhon Wat, and the ancient capital of the Cambodian empire. One hour's gentle canter through a grand old forest brought us to the vicinity of the temple, and here we found our progress materially arrested by huge blocks of freestone, which were now half buried in the soil. A few minutes more, and we came upon a broad flight of stone steps, guarded by colossal stone lions, one of which had been overthrown, and lay among the débris. My pony cleared this obstacle, and then with a series of scrambling leaps brought me to the long cruciform terrace which is carried on arches across the moat. This moat is a wide one, and has been banked with strong retaining walls of iron-conglomerate. The view from the stone platform far surpassed my expectations. The vast proportions of the temple filled me with a feeling of profound awe, such as I experienced some years afterwards when sailing beneath the shade of the gigantic precipices of the Upper Yang-tsze.

. . . I believe that a richer field for research has never been laid open to those who take an interest in the great building races of the East than that revealed by the discovery of the magnificent remains which the ancient Cambodians have left behind them. Their stone cities lie buried in malarious forests and jungles, and though many of them have been examined, not a few are still wholly unexplored; and indeed it is impossible for anyone who has not visited the spot to form a true estimate of the wealth and resources of the ancient Cambodians, or of the howling wilderness to which their country has been reduced by the ravages of war, the destructive encroachments of tropical jungle, . . . The disappearance of this once splendid civilisation, and the relapse of the people into a primitiveness bordering, in some quarters, on the condition of the lower animals, seems to prove that man is a retrogressive as well as a progressive being, and that he may probably relapse into the simple forms of organic life from which he is supposed by some to have originally sprung.

. . . We spent several days at the ruined city of Nakhon, on the verge of the native jungle, and amidst a forest of magnificent trees. Here we were surrounded on every side by ruins as multitudinous as they were gigantic; one building alone covered an area of vast extent, and was crowned with fifty-one stone towers. Each tower was sculptured to represent a four-faced Buddha, or Brahma, and thus 204 colossal sphinx-like countenances gazed benignly towards the cardinal points—all full of that expression of purity and repose which Buddhists so love to portray, and all wearing diadems of the most chaste design above their unruffled stony brows. At the outer gate of this city, I experienced a sort of modern 'battle of the apes'. Reared high above the gateway stood a series of subordinate towers, having a single larger one in their centre, whose apex again displayed to us the four benign faces of the ancient god. The image was partly concealed beneath parasitic plants, which twined their clustering fibres in a rude garland around the now neglected head. When I attempted to photograph this object, a tribe of black apes, wearing white beards, came hooting along the branches of the overhanging tree, swinging and shaking the boughs, so as to render my success impossible. A party of French sailors, who were assisting the late Captain de Lagrée in his researches into the Cambodian ruins, came up opportunely, and sent a volley among my mischievous opponents; whereupon they disappeared with what haste they might, and fled away till their monkey jargon was lost in the recesses of the forest.'

John Thomson, The Straits of Malacca, Indo-China, and China; or, Ten Years' Travels, Adventures, and Residence Abroad, 1875

Appendices

Appendix I
Suggested Itineraries

Some itineraries are suggested to help you plan a visit to Angkor. Each one is divided into 'morning' and 'afternoon' trips and takes into consideration the climate, distances, and condition of the roads. Refer to maps on pages 76, 80 and 177 to help you plan your itineraries.

The ideal sequence for following the historic and artistic development of the Khmers is to visit the sites in chronological order. Even though this is not very practical, if one has the time and the desire, such a tour is recommended. The sites at Angkor and its environs in chronological order are:

Ninth Century: Roluos: Prah Kō (879), Bakong (881), Lolei (893)

Tenth Century: Phnom Krom, Phnom Bakheng, Prasat Kravan (921), Baksei Chamkrong (947), East Mebon (952), Pre Rup (961), Banteay Srei (967), Thma Bay Kaek, Prasat Bei

Eleventh Century: Kleangs (North and South), Phimeanakas, Ta Keo, Baphuon (1060), West Mebon, West Baray

Twelfth Century–early Thirteenth Century: Chau Say Tevoda, Thommanon, Angkor Wat (1113–50), Ta Prohm, Prah Khan (1191), Banteay Kdei, Banteay Samre, Neak Pean, Krol Kō, Prah Palilay, Srah Srang, Prasat Suor Prat, Ta Som, Terraces (Elephants, Leper King), Angkor Thom, Bayon, Ta Prohm Kel, Chapel of the Hospital

The 'classic' tour of Angkor set out by the French includes two routes—the little circuit ('Le Petit Cirque') and the large circuit ('Le Grand Cirque')—based on the road system.

THE LITTLE CIRCUIT

Angkor Wat, Ta Prohm Kel, Bakheng, Baksei Chamkrong, Thma Bay Kaek, Prasat Bei, Angkor Thom, Bayon, Baphuon, Phimeanakas, Prah Palilay, Tep Pranam, Terraces (Elephants, Leper King), Prasat Suor Prat, Kleangs (North and South), Chau Say Tevoda, Thommanon, Spean Thma, Chapel of the Hospital, Ta Keo, Ta Prohm, Banteay Kdei (for the last two, enter at the west and depart at the east), Srah Srang, Prasat Kravan.

THE LARGE CIRCUIT

Angkor Wat, Angkor Thom, Prah Khan (enter at the west and depart at the north), Neak Pean, Krol Kō, Ta Som, East Mebon, Pre Rup, Srah Srang.

(preceding page) *Celestial nymphs dancing on lotuses, the Bayon*

The following itineraries are based on the number of days available to see the sites:

ONE MORNING
Angkor Wat, Gate of Angkor Thom, Bayon, Ta Prohm, Srah Srang.

ONE AFTERNOON
Gate of Angkor Thom, Bayon, Ta Prohm, Srah Srang, Angkor Wat.

ONE DAY
AM Srah Srang (sunrise), Pre Rup, Neak Pean, Prah Khan, Terraces (Elephants, Leper King).
PM Bayon, Ta Prohm, Ta Keo, Gate of Angkor Thom, Angkor Wat (sunset).

TWO DAYS
1. AM Baksei Chamkrong, Bayon, Baphuon, Terraces (Elephants, Leper King), Tep Pranam, Prah Palilay.
   PM Banteay Kdei, Srah Srang, Ta Prohm, Ta Keo, Gate of Angkor Thom, Phnom Bakheng (sunset).
2. AM Prasat Kravan, Pre Rup, Ta Som, Neak Pean, Prah Khan.
   PM Angkor Wat.

THREE DAYS
1. AM Baksei Chamkrong, Thma Bay Kaek, Prasat Bei, Bayon, Baphuon, Prah Palilay, Tep Pranam, Terraces (Elephants, Leper King).
   PM Banteay Kdei, Srah Srang, Ta Prohm, Ta Keo, Chau Say Tevoda, Thommanon, Gate of Angkor Thom, Phnom Bakheng (sunset).
2. AM Prasat Kravan, Pre Rup, Ta Som, Neak Pean, Krol Kō, Prah Khan.
   PM Roluos (Bakong, Prah Kō, Lolei), Phnom Krom.
3. AM Banteay Srei, Banteay Samre, East Mebon.
   PM Angkor Wat (sunset).

FOUR DAYS
1. AM Bayon, Terraces (Elephants, Leper King), Kleangs (North and South), Prasat Suor Prat, Tep Pranam, Prah Palilay, Phimeanakas.
   PM Baksei Chamkrong, Thma Bay Kaek, Prasat Bei, Baphuon, Gate of Angkor Thom, Thommanon, Chau Say Tevoda, Spean Thma, Chapel of the Hospital, Phnom Bakheng (sunset).

2. *AM* Ta Keo, Ta Prohm, Banteay Kdei, Srah Srang, Prasat Kravan.
   PM Angkor Wat (sunset).
3. *AM* Pre Rup, Ta Som, Neak Pean, Krol Kō, Prah Khan.
   PM West Mebon, Phnom Krom (sunset).
4. *AM* Banteay Srei, Banteay Samre, East Mebon.
   PM Roluos (Lolei, Prah Kō, Bakong at sunset).

FIVE DAYS

1. *AM* Angkor Wat (sunrise), Ta Prohm Kel.
   PM Roluos (Bakong, Prah Kō, Lolei), Bakheng (sunset).
2. *AM* Baksei Chamkrong, Thma Bay Kaek, Prasat Bei, Gate of Angkor Thom, Baphuon, Terraces (Elephants, Leper King), Tep Pranam, Prah Palilay, Phimeanakas, Kleangs (North and South), Prasat Suor Prat.
   PM Prah Khan, Neak Pean, Krol Kō, Ta Som, Pre Rup (sunset).
3. *AM* Banteay Srei.
   PM Banteay Samre, East Mebon.
4. *AM* Ta Prohm, Ta Keo, Chapel of the Hospital, Spean Thma, Chau Say Tevoda, Thommanon.
   PM Prasat Kravan, Banteay Kdei, Srah Srang, Angkor Wat (sunset).
5. *AM* Phnom Krom, West Mebon.
   PM Bayon.

Appendix II
Comparative Chronology of the Khmer and Other Civilizations

BC
c 5000–0
CAM: Early society
WEST: Stonehenge (2200–1700)
        Parthenon (447–433)

AD
0–100
SEA: Indianization
IND: Sāñcī stupa; Amaravati stupa
CH: End of Western Han Dynasty
WEST: Birth of Christ
        Ptolemy's *Geography*
        Colosseum (Rome) (72–80)

200
CAM: Funan
SEA: Early state of Champa (200)
        Pyu kingdom (Burma) (250)
IND: Pallava Dynasty

300
SEA: Oc Eo (Vietnam)
IND: Gupta Dynasty (320–600)
CH: Dunhuang Caves (336)

400
IND: Wall-paintings at Ajanta
        Wall-paintings at Sigiriya (Sri Lanka)

CAM: Cambodia, CH: China, IND: India, SEA: Southeast Asia, WEST: the West

500

CAM: Zhenla
IND: Ellura Caves
WEST: Hagia Sophia (Constantinople) (532–7)

600

CAM: Sambor Prei Kuk
     Iśanavarman I
     Jayavarman I (645–81)
SEA: Dvāravatī Kingdom
     Srivijaya Dynasty (c 680–1287)
IND: Mamallapurmam Temples (625–75)
CH: Tang dynasty (618–906)

700

CAM: Upper and Lower Zhenla
SEA: Śailendras Dynasty (750)
     Borobudur (Java)
IND: Pala Dynasty

800

CAM: Jayavarman II (802–50)
     Jayavarman III (850–77)
     Indravarman I (877–89)
     Yaśovarman I (893–c 900)
SEA: Pegu (880)
IND: Temple of Kailāsa at Ellura (800)
WEST: Charlemagne, Emperor of the West (800)
     Beginning of the Norman invasions
     First cathedral at Cologne (Germany) (873)
     Siege of Paris by the Normans (885)

900

CAM: Harshavarman (c 900–22)
     Iśanavarman II (922–7)
     Jayavarman IV (921–41)
     Harshavarman II (941–4)
     Rājendravarman (944–68)
     Jayavarman V (968–1001)

IND: Chola Empire (900–1170)
CH: The Five Dynasties (907–60)
Northern Song Dynasty (960–1125)

1000

CAM: Udayadityavarman I (1001–2)
Jayaviravarman (1002–11)
Sūryavarman I (1002–50)
Udayadityavarman II (1050–66)
Jayavarman VI (1080–1107)
WEST: Conquest of Sicily by knights of Normandy (1010)
St Mark's, Venice (1042–85)
Westminster Abbey (1052–65)
Norman Conquest of England (1066)
Winchester Cathedral (1079)
Durham Cathedral (1096)

1100

CAM: Dharanidravarman I (1107–13)
Sūryavarman II (1113–c 1150)
Yaśovarman II (1150–65)
Tribhuvanadityavarman (1165–77)
Jayavarman VII (1181–c 1219)
SEA: Chams seize Angkor (1177)
IND: Conquest of Northern India by Mongols (1192–6)
CH: Southern Song (1127–1276)
WEST: Notre-Dame de Paris (1163–1235)
Oxford University (1167)

1200

CAM: Indravarman II (1220–43)
Jayavarman VIII (c 1243–95)
SEA: Sukhothai Kingdom (Thailand)
Lan Na Kingdom (Thailand)
IND: Temple of Karnak (Egypt)
CH: Yuan Dynasty (1270–1368)
Mongol conquest of China
Zhou Daguan at Angkor (1296–7)
WEST: Magna Carta (1215)

The Great Interregnum (1250–73)
Marco Polo to the court of Kublai Khan (1271–95)

1300

CAM: Srindravarman (1300–07)
Jayavarmadiparamesvara (1327–)
Angkor seized by the Thais (1353)
SEA: Ayutthaya kingdom (1350–1767)
CH: Ming Dynasty (1368–1644)
WEST: Beginning of the Hundred Years' War (1337)

1400

CAM: Thais sack Angkor (1431)
CH: Imperial Palace and Temple of Heaven at Beijing (1421)

Kāla, *a mythical creature who swallowed his body,*
is placed over doorways to temples and serves as a guardian

Appendix III
Chronology of the Monuments

NINTH CENTURY
Roluos:
879–	Prah Kō
881–	Bakong
893–	Lolei

TENTH CENTURY
—	Bakheng
—	Phnom Krom
921–	Prasat Kravan
947	Baksei Chamkrong
952–	East Mebon
961–	Pre Rup
967–	Banteay Srei
—	Prasat Bei
—	Thma Bay Kaek
—	Kleangs (North and South)

11TH CENTURY
1000–1025	Ta Keo
—	Phimeanakas
1050–1066	Baphuon
—	West Mebon
—	West Baray

12TH–13TH CENTURY
1113–1150	Angkor Wat
1150–	Chau Say Tevoda
1150–	Thommanon
1150–1175	Banteay Samre
1186–	Ta Prohm
—	Banteay Kdei
1190–1210	Neak Pean

1190–1210	Ta Som
1190–1210	Srah Srang
1190–1210	Angkor Thom
1190–1210	Bayon
1190–1210	Terrace of the Elephants
1190–1210	Terrace of the Leper King
—	Krol Kō
—	Prah Palilay
—	Prasat Suor Prat
1191–	Prah Khan
—	Ta Prom Kel
—	Chapel of the Hospital

Appendix IV
Chronology of Cambodian Kings

Dates of Reign	Name of King	Posthumous Name	Monuments
802–850	Jayavarman II	Paramesvara	Kulen
850–877	Jayavarman III	Vishnuloka	
877–889	Indravarman I	Iśvaraloka	Prah Kō, Bakong
889–900+	Yaśovarman I	Paramasivaloka	Lolei, Bakheng, Phnom Krom, Kravan
900–944+	Harshavarman I	Rudraloka	
		Iśanavarman II	Paramarudraloka
921–941	Jayavarman IV	Paramasivapada	
941–944	Harshavarman II	Vrahmaloka or Brahmaloka	
944–968	Rājendravarman II	Śivaloka	Baksei Chamkrong, East Mebon, Pre Rup
968–1001	Jayavarman V	Paramasivaloka	
1001–1002	Udayadityavarman I		
1002–1011	Jayaviravarman		
1002–1050	Sūryavarman I	Nirvanapala la	Ta Keo, Phimeanakas
1050–1066	Udayadityavarman II		Baphuon, West Mebon, West Baray?
1066–1080	Harshavarman III		Sadasivapada
1080–1107	Jayavarman VI		Paramakaivalyapada
1107–1113	Dharanindravarman I	Paramanishkalapada	
1113–c 1150	Sūryavarman II	Paramavishnuloka	Angkor Wat, Chau Say Tevoda, Thommanon, Banteay Samre
1150–1160	Dharanindravarman II		Paramanishkalapada
1160–1165	Yaśovarman II		
1165–1177	Tribhuvanadityavarman		

1181–1219	Jayavarman VII	Mahaparamasaugata	Ta Prohm, Banteay Kdei, Neak Pean, Ta Som, Srah Srang, Angkor Thom, Bayon, Terrace of the Elephants, Terrace of the Leper King, Krol Kō, Prah Palilay, Prah Khan, Prasat Suor Prat
1220–1243		Indravarman II	
1243–1295		Jayavarman VIII (abdicated)	Paramesvarapada
1296–			
1300–1307		Srindravarman (abdicated)	
1308–1327		Indrajayavarman Srindrajayavarman	
1327		Jayavarmadiparamesvara	
1330–1353		Paramathakemaraja	
1371–		Hou-eul-na	
1404		Samtac Prah Phaya	
1405		Samtac Chao Phaya Phing-ya	
1405–1409		Nippean-bat	
1409–1416		Lampong, or Lampang Paramaraja	
1416–1425		Sorijovong, Sorijong, or Lambang	
1425–1429		Barom Racha, or Gamkhat Ramadhapati	
1429–1431		Thommo-Soccorach, or Dharmasoka	
1432–		Ponha Yat, or Gam Yat	

Appendix V
The Main Divinities Depicted in Khmer Art and Their Characteristics

Name:	Agni (God of Fire)
Heads:	2
Arms:	4
Attributes:	fan, axe, torch, ladle
Mount:	rhinoceros

Name:	Brahmā (The Creator)
Heads:	4 (faces)
Arms:	4
Attributes:	disc, ladle, book, rosary, vase, fly whisk, sceptre
Mount:	goose
Spouse:	Sarasvatī

Name:	Ganeśa (God of Wisdom)
Arms:	2 or 4
Char:	elephant head with corpulent human body
Attributes:	elephant goad, noose
Mount:	rat

Name:	Indra (God of the Sky)
Char:	tiara or turban; elaborate clothes and jewellery
Attributes:	thunderbolt, disc, elephant goad, axe
Mount:	elephant (often three-headed)

Name:	Kāma (God of Love)
Attributes:	floral bow and arrows
Mount:	parrot
Spouse:	Rati

Name:	Kubera (God of Wealth)
Char:	fat dwarf, crown and jewellery, money bags nearby
Attributes:	lemon or pomegranate; mongoose spitting jewels
Mount:	horse

A stone god at an entrance to Angkor Thom

Name:	Lakṣmī (Goddess of Beauty), sometimes called Śrī (Goddess of Good Fortune)
Arms:	2 or 4
Char:	appears on a lotus pedestal, often attended by an elephant on each side
Attributes:	lotus blossom; conch, disc, and club (attributes of Viṣṇu)
Spouse:	Viṣṇu

Name:	Pārvatī (Daughter of the Mountain); sometimes called Umā ('the gracious one') or Durgā (fierce aspect; mount: tiger)
Arms:	2 or 4
Char:	chignon with curls; often on a lotus pedestal
Attributes:	lotus, rosary, vase; trident of Śiva
Mount:	lion
Spouse:	Śiva

Name:	Śiva (The Destroyer)
Arms:	4
Char:	chignon with curls, third frontal eye; sometimes bare torso wrapped with cord emulating a serpent; often represented in the form of a *liṅga*
Attributes:	trident
Mount:	bull
Spouse:	Pārvatī (Umā)

Name:	Skanda (God of War)
Heads:	6
Arms:	6
Char:	tiara or hair divided into three locks and knotted on top of head; depicted as archer at Angkor Wat
Attributes:	double thunderbolt, sword, trident
Mount:	peacock

Name:	Sūrya (God of Sun)
Char:	long tunic, high boots, often with the moon
Attributes:	lotus (sometimes)
Mount:	chariot drawn by seven horses

Name:	Viṣṇu (The Preserver)
Arms:	4
Char:	*sampot* with a belt; cylindrical headdress (early), diadem (late)

Attributes: conch, disc, club and a ball or lotus
Mount: Garuḍa
Spouse: Lakṣmī

Name: Yama (God of Justice and the Underworld)
Arms: 8 (usually)
Attributes: clubs
Mount: buffalo

Further Reading

GENERAL BACKGROUND AND HISTORICAL

Briggs, Lawrence, 'The Ancient Khmer Empire', *Transactions of the American Philosophical Society*, Vol 41, Pt 1 (1951)

Chandler, David, *A History of Cambodia* (Westview Press, Boulder, Colorado, 1983; rev ed Colorado and Oxford, England, 1992, Silkworm Books, Chiang Mai, Thailand, 1993)

Chou Ta-Kuan (Zhou Daguan), *The Customs of Cambodia*, 2nd ed, Paul Pelliot, trans (The Siam Society, Bangkok, 1992)

Cœdès, George, *The Indianized States of Southeast Asia,* Susan Brown Cowing, trans (East–West Center Press, Honolulu, 1968)

Dagens, Bruno, *Angkor: La Fôret de Pierre* (Découvertes Gallimard Archéologie, Paris, 1989)

White, Peter T, 'The Temples of Angkor, Ancient Glory in Stone', *National Geographic*, Vol 161, No 5, 1982, pp 552–589

THE ART OF THE KHMERS

Boisselier, Jean, *Trends in Khmer Art*, Natasha Eilenberg, trans and ed (Cornell University, Studies on Southeast Asia, Ithaca, New York, 1989)

Cœdès, George, *Angkor: An Introduction*, Emily Floyd Gardiner, trans and ed (Oxford University Press, New York and Hong Kong, 1963)

Freeman, Michael, *A Golden Souvenir of Angkor* (Pacific Rim Press, Hong Kong, 1992)

Freeman, Michael and Roger Warner, *Angkor: The Hidden Glories* (Houghton Mifflin, Boston, 1990)

Giteau, Madeleine, *Khmer Sculpture and the Angkor Civilization* (Harry N Abrams, New York, 1965; Thames and Hudson, London, 1965)

Groslier, Bernard-Philippe & Jacques Arthaud, *Angkor, Art and Civilization* (rev ed Praeger, New York, 1966; Thames and Hudson, London, 1966)

Jacques, Claude, *Angkor* (Bordas, Paris, 1990) [French text]

Macdonald, Malcolm, *Angkor: and the Khmers* (Oxford University Press, London, 1987)

Rawson, Philip, *The Art of Southeast Asia, Cambodia Vietnam Thailand Laos Burma Java Bali* (Thames and Hudson, London, 1967; rep Asia Books, Bangkok, 1990)

Rooney, Dawn, *Khmer Ceramics* (Oxford University Press, Kuala Lumpur, Malaysia, 1984)

Travel, Personal Accounts

Lewis, Norman, *A Dragon Apparent: Travels in Cambodia, Laos and Vietnam* (rep Eland Books, London, 1982)

Madsen, Axel, *Silk Roads: The Asian Adventures of Clara & André Malraux* (I B Tauris, London, 1990)

Mouhot, M Henri, *Travels in the Central Parts of Indo-China (Siam), Cambodia, and Laos, During the Years 1858, 1859, and 1860*, 2 vols (John Murray, London, 1864; rep White Lotus, Bangkok, 1986)

Thomson, John, *The Straits of Malacca, Siam and Indo-China Travels and Adventures of a Nineteenth-century Photographer* (Sampson Low, Marston, Low and Searle, London, 1875; rep Oxford University Press, Singapore, 1993)

Vincent, Frank, *The Land of the White Elephant: Sights and Scenes in South-East Asia 1871–1872*, (Harper & Brothers, New York, 1873; rep Oxford University Press, Singapore, 1988)

Glossary

Airāvata A multi-headed elephant; Indra's mount

Amitābha Represented in Khmer art as a seated Buddha meditating; depicted on the headdress of a bodhisattva

amṛta The drink of immortality that was created by the Churning of the Ocean of Milk

Ananta see Vāsuki

anastylosis A method of restoring a monument distinguished by rebuilding the structure using the original methods and materials

Angkor (Kh) ('city or capital') An ancient capital in Cambodia that was the main centre of the Khmer Empire from AD 802 to 1432

Angkor Thom (Kh) The 'great' city built in the late 12th century by Jayavarman VII. It is located north of Angkor Wat with the temple of the Bayon at its centre

apsarā (pl *apsarās*) A female divinity; heavenly dancer; celestial nymph

asura A demon with god-like power

avatāras ('descent') Refers to the descent of Viṣṇu in bodily form from heaven to be reincarnated on earth

Balarāma The elder twin brother of Kṛṣṇa; Viṣṇu's eighth *avatāras*

baluster A short post or pillar in a series that supports a rail and forms a balustrade

Banteay (Kh) ('fortress') The name given to a temple with an enclosing wall

baray (Kh) ('lake') A large man-made body of water surrounded by banks of earth; reservoir

bas-relief A sculpture in low relief with the figures projecting less than half the true proportions from the background

bodhisattva In Mahāyāna Buddhism, a compassionate being who could become a Buddha but postpones his *nirvāṇa* and elects to stay on earth to help mankind achieve enlightenment

Brahmanism The early religion of India that emanated from Vedism

Buddha An enlightened being

Cambodia A country in Southeast Asia bounded by Laos, Thailand, Vietnam and the Gulf of Thailand

causeway A raised road across a body of water

Champa An ancient Indianized state and rival of the Khmer Empire. It was situated in an area corresponding approximately to present-day south and central Vietnam. It existed from the second century to the 15th century

Chenla see Zhenla

corbel A method of spanning an opening used by the Khmers for arches. It consists of an overlapping arrangement of stones, each course projecting beyond the one below

deva (feminine = *devi*) A deity; celestial being

devarāja A cult instituted by Jayavarman II in AD 802 in Cambodia; based on the tenet that the king was an emanation of a god and would be reunited with that god upon death; usually represented in Khmer art by a phallus symbolizing the spiritual and royal essence of the Khmer king

dvārapāla A guardian often standing and holding a club or mace; sculpted in the round and frequently at the entrance to a temple

Dvāravatī A Mon kingdom in Thailand from approximately the sixth or seventh century to the 11th century

Funan A Chinese name for an ancient Indianized kingdom that seems to have been the predecessor to Angkor; located in the lower Mekong basin; although it existed in the first century AD, its zenith was the fifth century; in the seventh century it was eclipsed by the state of Zhenla

Garuḍa A mythical creature depicted in Khmer art with the arms and torso of a human and the beak, wings, legs and claws of an eagle; an enemy of the *nāgas*; Viṣṇu's mount

gopura An elaborate gateway to a temple in south India; it serves as an entrance pavilion in walls enclosing a temple; this book uses the term 'entry tower' in place of 'gopura'

haṁsa A sacred goose; Brahmā's mount

Hanumān A mythical monkey from the *Rāmāyana*; chief of the army of monkeys

Hari-Hara ('Hari' = Viṣṇu; 'Hara' = Śiva) A deity who is a combination of these two gods and represents a synthesis of the two Hindu cults. The figure is depicted with Viṣṇu's tiara on one side and Śiva's plaited locks on the other and holding the main attributes of both gods

Hīnayāna Buddhism The 'Lesser Vehicle'; became predominant religion in Cambodia in the 15th century; more commonly called Theravāda Buddhism

Hinduism The religion and social system of the Hindus; popular in Cambodia particularly from the first century to the 13th century

Kailāsa One of the summits of the Himalayas

kāla A mythical monster with the characteristics of a wide grinning face, bulging eyes, claws and pointed ears

Kalkin see Viṣṇu

Khmer (Kh) The ancient indigenous people of Cambodia

Lakṣmaṇa The brother of Rāma

laterite A residual product of rock decay abundant in the soil of Cambodia and Northeastern Thailand; characterized by a porous texture and a red colour; hardens on exposure to air; used as a building material, particularly for foundations of Khmer temples

liṅga A representation of the male organ of generation, a symbol of Śiva and his role in creation

lintel A crossbeam resting on two upright posts. On a Khmer temple the lintel is above the door or window opening, directly below the pediment

lokapāla One of the guardians of the four cardinal points

Lokeśvara ('Lord of the World') The name is often used in Asia for the compassionate bodhisattva Avalokiteśvara

Mahābhārata One of the great Indian epics. It describes a civil war in north India

Mahāyāna Buddhism The 'Greater Vehicle'; a school of Buddhism; flourished in Cambodia, particularly in the late 12th and early 13th centuries

makara A mythical water monster with the body of a crocodile and the trunk of an elephant

Meru A mythical mountain at the centre of the Universe and home of the gods; the axis of the world around which the continents and the oceans are ordered

Mucilinda The *nāga* king who sheltered the Buddha while he was meditating during a storm

nāga A mythical serpent and progenitor of the Khmer race; has the characteristics of a stylized cobra; generally multi-headed; the spirit of the waters

Nandi A bull; Śiva's mount

nirvāṇa The 'Extinction' and final liberation from the cycle of rebirths

Pali A language derived from Vedic Sanskrit

pediment The triangular upper portion of a wall above the portico

phnom (Kh) 'mountain or hill'

pilaster A column used on the side of an open doorway that projects slightly from the wall

prah (Kh) 'Sacred, holy'

Prasat (Kh) A sanctuary in the form of a tower

quincunx A square platform supporting five towers—one in each corner and one in the centre

Rāhu A demon depicted with a monster's head

rākṣasa A demon who lives in Laṅkā with Rāvaṇa

Rāma The hero of the *Rāmāyaṇa*; the seventh *avatāras* of Viṣṇu

Rāmāyana An Indian epic describing the story of Rāma and Sītā

Rāvaṇa King of the *rākṣasas* depicted with ten heads and twenty arms. His abduction
of Sītā and battle against Rāma are the essential parts of the *Rāmāyana*
śakti The energy of a feminine deity who is regarded as the consort of the god
sampot (Kh) A Cambodian garment worn as a covering for the lower body
Sītā Rāma's wife and heroine of the *Rāmāyana*
spean (Kh) 'bridge'
srah (Kh) 'pond'
srei (Kh) 'woman'
Sugrīva The monkey king in the *Rāmāyana*
ta (Kh) 'ancestor'
Theravāda Buddhism The 'Doctrine of the Elders' representing the traditional Pali
heritage of early Buddhism (*see* Hīnāyana Buddhism)
Tonle Sap (Kh) ('sweet water') A freshwater sea in western Cambodia that is linked
with the Mekong River by the Tonle Sap River
-varman (Kh) The 'protected', the victorious; the suffix is often attached to the names
of Khmer kings
Vāsuki The serpent upon which Viṣṇu reclines or sits. It served as a rope when the
Ocean of Milk was churned by the gods and demons. It is sometimes called
Ananta or Śeṣa
wat A Thai word meaning 'temple'
yakṣa A mythical and supernatural being; may be good or evil
Zhenla (Chenla) An ancient Chinese name for a state in Cambodia that existed from
the sixth century to the eighth century

Index

Stone god holding the body of a serpent at the royal city of Angkor Thom